WINNING THE ATHLETIC MENTAL GAME

33 Interviews with America's Top Coaches
and Performance Psychologists on
Gaining Your Competitive Edge

EDITED BY JOHN SIKES JR.

CHAMPIONSHIP
PERFORMANCE

Charlotte, North Carolina 28277

Cover photo: University of Wisconsin Ice Hockey Coach Mark Johnson
Courtesy of Jeff Miller, University of Wisconsin-Madison.

ISBN-13: 978-0615620060

Championship Performance
10612 D Providence Road Suite 262
Charlotte, NC 28277
Phone: (704) 321-9198
Fax: (704) 321-0203
www.championshipperform.com

CHAMPIONSHIP
PERFORMANCE

ACKNOWLEDGEMENTS

I would to thank everyone involved in making this book possible.

To Anver Suleiman, who gave me my first break out of college and for having a vision to take sport psychology principles to athletic coaches.

To Wayne Cooper for production assistance and inspiration.

To Brandi Rabon for proofing and making this book a better read.

To all the coaches and sports psychologists who took the time to provide such great interviews.

To my parents, John and Sandy Sikes, for their support over the years.

To my children, Hope and Joshua, for challenging me in ways I never thought possible.

To my wife Kate, for always standing by me.

For God - Father, Son and Spirit for Life, Salvation, and Peace.

Matthew 11:28

Jeremiah 33-3

- John Sikes Jr.

CONTENTS

PART 1:
THE COACHING INTERVIEWS

v

PART 2:
THE SPORT PSYCHOLOGY INTERVIEWS

INTRODUCTION

15 years ago in the fall of 1996, the *Championship Performance* coaches journal was launched. Originally titled "The Mental Edge", we quickly changed the name to *Championship Performance*, the name of the company who published it, because that was what the journal was all about - winning championships.

Championship Performance has become the definitive resource for coaches on performance psychology, leadership, mental toughness, motivation, and team building.

Thousands of coaches over the years have obtained the mental edge on the competition reading the coaching journal. I've had the pleasure of editing every single issue.

You are about to read 33 of the best interviews conducted for the journal. These run the gamut on everything it takes to build and sustain a championship program. This is the cumulative wisdom of coaches who have won over 50 combined national titles in their respective sports.

In this book, 21 of America's most successful coaches and 12 of the most respected performance psychologists offer their very best insights on what it takes to win in today's competitive environment. They have helped thousands of athletes realize their athletic dreams.

For tons more great monthly insights on gaining the mental edge on the competition, you can subscribe to the *Championship Performance* coaches journal. For more information, please visit: www.championshipperform.com.

- PART 1 -

THE
COACHING
INTERVIEWS

- 1 -

LOU HOLTZ: ESSENTIALS OF COACHING LEADERSHIP

ESPN analyst and former Head Football Coach at Notre Dame, Arkansas, and South Carolina, Lou Holtz led the Fighting Irish to a national championship in 1988. He is author of 8 books including the best seller "Winning Every Day: A Game Plan for Success."

You've been able to quickly turn around losing programs wherever you have coached. What common problems did you encounter when you took over?

Whenever you go into losing situations the common problem is that you will find a group of guys who don't have a lot of confidence. But the predominant thing is there aren't any core values. There is an "anything goes" mentality if you don't have any core values.

What I mean by core values is: "what do we believe in as a family? Do you believe in each other, trust one another, and do you have commitment and caring?"

These are things that everybody on your football team should have. Then if one of your core values is to do everything to the best of your ability, the team is going to improve and get better.

And when they get better, that is where the turnaround begins. You can pinpoint one hundred different things on losing programs, but I think core values are probably the most important things, and they are probably the least talked about as well.

What advice would you have for a coach, of any sport, who is taking over a program with no winning tradition?

You have to establish a winning tradition by going through four stages.

The first thing you have to do is learn how to compete. You learn how to compete and come close to winning. In the second stage you learn how to win.

The third stage you learn how to handle winning. Once you start winning, there are problems also. You can't get content when you have a little bit of success.

The fourth stage is you take the program to a championship level. Most teams do not win because they don't execute the fundamentals. Most teams, in any sport, beat themselves more than anything else. I think attitude is critical. Establishing a proper attitude is important, and it starts with your attitude as head coach.

How did you keep the South Carolina team focused and on track after the 0-11 first season?

Some of our seniors commented the other day, saying that even though we were 0 and 11 and lost all our games, we didn't lose the team.
I didn't jump around and say, "well, we are going to try this or we are going to try that". I had a plan. I believed in the plan. All we had to do was implement it and adopt the core values. And if we adopted the core values, we would start getting better and then stop beating ourselves. The tougher the situation, the closer the group must be. Everything goes back to core values.

What is one key to keeping the program running at a consistently high level?

You could write a book on this one, but I'll try to give you one main thing. The main question to ask the players is, "are you satisfied?" You know we have just won two Outback Bowls, and we beat Ohio State University. Are we satisfied? - No. I am not, and I hope the players aren't. We are pleased with where we are, but we are not satisfied. And I think you ought to approach it every year like you are coming off a 0 and 11 year by staying hungry.

How do you develop leadership skills - in yourself and in your players?

I count on our juniors and seniors. We have a big brother program where every freshman that comes in has an upper classman who tutors him, teaches him and answers his questions.

Predominantly, the upperclassman is there to teach the freshman how we do things. And I ask every underclassman, particularly juniors, to watch how the seniors do things. If we have a messy locker room, I will get on the seniors. They should handle that. I think that you have to give people responsibility, and the only way that they are going to develop that leadership is if they feel that it is their team.

Somebody can appoint you the head football coach. They can give you the title. But what they can't do is name you the leader. Nobody can give you the title of leader. The title leader must be earned. And the only way you become a leader is if: 1) you have a vision, and 2) you have a plan on how to get there.

I think the players have to accept you as a leader. First, they have to accept that you are going in the direction that they want to go. Second, they must believe that you are capable of taking them to where your vision is.

Describe your thoughts on motivation and is there any benefit to a half-time pep talk.

Motivation comes down to "what do we have to do to get there?" I ask these two questions: "Why is this game important, and what do we have to do to win it?" You go from your heart on that. I am not a great one for giving a pep talk.

If we are behind at half-time, I'm not going to rant and rave. I can do that on Monday or Sunday or when I see them next.

I am going to try to break it down. Let's say that we are behind by 24 points. I want them to look at the situation in a positive light. I don't want them thinking that the deficit seems like it is insurmountable or too large to overcome.

For example, I would say, "number one, we are averaging 32 points a game. We are behind 24 to nothing. Now dog gone it, you can't convince me that offensively we shouldn't be able to go out and score 14 points. There is no reason in this world we can't - we are averaging 32". "O.K., now there is no reason our kicking game should not be able to set up a touchdown by somehow blocking a punt or running a kick back, because we work hard on that in practice. And I know our defense is going to step it up and set up one touchdown. Now we have 28 and they have 24."

Conversely, if you are ahead by 24, then let's keep doing it. Let's win the 3rd quarter. If we win the 3rd quarter, you will eat hot-dogs, drink cokes and watch your scout teamers play the 4th quarter.
Finally, I don't stress winning. I stress playing as well as we can. The rest takes care of itself.

Football is really the ultimate team sport. Everyone has to pull together for the greater good. Over your years of coaching, can you identify some common factors of teams that had great "team chemistry" and conversely, reasons why some teams failed to come together as a unit?

I always tell the players that everybody needs somebody. There are all kinds of Halls of Fame, but I have never seen a monument built to a team. You can't have a bad attitude on the team. Who are the players with a bad attitude? They are the ones that think they are never wrong, they hold a grudge, they are selfish, petty, and they want all of the credit. You can't have that. The team goal is more important than your individual goal.

There is a whole list of things that I go over with them on a consistent basis. Team chemistry really comes together when everybody shares the same core values. You don't have to like one another, you don't have to party with one another, you don't have to eat with one another, you don't have to share the same religion. You don't even have to share the same philosophy of life, but you must share the same core values, which are trust, commitment and caring.

What is the best advice someone ever gave you as a young coach?

I had just got hired at NC State, and they had only won a few games in the previous three years. Recruiting was difficult. I went to the National Coaches Convention in Chicago. In the lobby, I ran into (former Navy and Temple coach) Wayne Hart. At this point, I'm tired and don't want to be there. Then he asked me, "are you the best person for the NC State job?" I said, " No. Look at all the great coaches out there." He looked right at me and said: "If you don't think that you are the best coach for NC State in the country, you ought to resign because you are just stealing their money. He said NC State thought that you were the best coach for the job - that's the reason they hired you, so you ought to think you are". I made up my mind if NC State was dumb enough to think that I was the best coach, then dog gone it I was going to act like it. From that point on I just took the mental approach that I was the best guy for the job.

Who was your biggest mentor?

Even though I never coached with him, (former Texas Coach) Darrell Royal was a huge influence on me and my approach and philosophy towards the game. I went down to visit him, and he spent a lot of time with me. I had 84 questions that I asked him, and he could not have been any kinder.

At the time, I was just a young assistant coach who had paid my way down there. They had just won the National Championship, but it was in the summer. He was in his office and told I had some questions I would like to ask. He was about to leave to play golf, but he told me to start asking. This was at 11:00 am and at 5:00 pm; we were still in his office. I asked him things like, "what do you do if you have a guy that will not conform?" He said you have to close ranks, pick up the rifle and march on. He said those guys are going to hurt you in the long run anyway. I have often looked back on that meeting for guidance. The way he had expressed himself was tremendous.

Is there a way to tell if a student athlete is self-motivated?

Not really, but the one thing that I look at is the kind of respect a young man shows for his parents in his home. Because if he doesn't respect his parents and show them due respect, then he is not going to respect authority, and he is going to have trouble with the dorm, trouble in the classroom and trouble accepting coaches.

In recruiting, we as coaches, have a tendency to answer all of the athlete's questions. I think you need to ask them some questions. What are your intentions? What is your greatest excitement? What is your biggest disappointment? What do you want to do? I think you can tell a lot if you ask questions. I have never learned anything by talking. I only learn by listening.

- 2 -

DAVID MARSH: TURNING DREAMS INTO 12 NATIONAL TITLES

David Marsh is the Director of Swim MAC Carolina, an elite swim training facility based in Charlotte, NC. While at Auburn University, he directed the Men and Women's teams to a combined 12 national titles.

When an athlete gets into a slump, do you usually back off or push them harder? Which strategy is usually more effective and why? What do you say to an athlete going through a downward spiral?

In our sport, a slump would mean they haven't improved their swim time in a long while. In that situation, you pull back to the basics. Usually a slump is an indication that an athlete is not focused on where they need to be. A lot of times, an athlete needs to evaluate their basic motivation. When his/her motivation is based on pleasing a parent or coach or some other form of external motivation that doesn't tie into his/her core values, he/she is in trouble. Assess the basics, including fundamental biomechanical things or routines in the day that may be sapping an athlete's energy.

Are there relationships that bring stress into their world so that they can't concentrate during practice?

In general, I gear them down more than charge forward. I want them to evaluate "Life 101" and "Athletics 101" and rebuild from there. People in slumps can usually maintain a semblance of their old level. They are having a hard time getting to that next step. The higher you get in any athletic venue, the steps to improvement are much smaller along the way. So it's important to focus on the measurable things- reassessing your goals and reviewing practical evaluation areas. Take a mental assessment as well. If you have an athlete who has shot up fast (improved rapidly), but didn't athletically mature along the way, he/she probably doesn't know a whole lot about how he (she) is really good. That's when the education process begins again.

How do you mentally prepare your athletes for a competition?

I want them smiling and relaxed before a race. I want them to do what they know they are capable of doing. They must strike a balance between being over hyped and ready. There are six sessions during a swim competition. The preliminaries are more important than finals for team scoring aspects, so you have to perform well in the morning. Having several swimmers reach the finals is more important than individual winners.

We talk about "energy conservation" at the beginning of the year. We want them to learn how to get up real high and enjoy and celebrate with their teammates for their accomplishments, but to also know how to relax after the one race is over. It can be something as simple as sitting down in the bleachers and stretching their legs after that initial good energy. When the first race is over and they are warming down, I want them to start thinking about the next race.

Becoming enthusiastic and later coming down is a skill that can be learned and is a key to success. I talk to the team about the types of music they listen to before a contest vs. after a meet. To psyche themselves up before a meet, they can listen to upbeat stuff, but on the ride back to the hotel and later that night, I instruct the coaches not to have on rocking music because I want them to get more cerebral and to relax and chill out.

Swimming is a tournament like atmosphere. We have to be ready to race again the next morning. When we go back to the hotel, I don't want them watching the replays of the evening finals because I don't want to get them excited again. After the team meal, I want them to go back to their rooms and relax so they can get to sleep sooner. We don't allow any parent visitation at night. They can do that in the morning or afternoon. We try to make sure the evenings before a meet are very calm.

Do you implement any specific goal setting programs? Are there daily training goals that each swimmer tries to attain?

First, we'll talk about what each individual's goals are. We'll review them. We'll have them do "dream sheets" where they will write out in long hand what their ideal race is. This will include mental preparation before the race, (e.g. "I'm stepping up to the blocks, adjusting my goggles, when I look across the field, I feel confident.")

We want each of our swimmers to have a "Plan A" ideal race before each competition. To help facilitate that in practice, the swimmers and the coaches will agree on certain sets they ought to be able to do if they are going to accomplish their goals. For example, a swimmer will need to do ten 50 yard sets under a certain time limit using a certain stroke tempo or count. Working backward, there are a host of things the athlete must do in the two months prior to set himself/herself up for accomplishing that goal.

Of course, each athlete has goal times. But those are broken down into minute parts, as far as splits are concerned meaning the different tempos they will need to use. In our sport, there is a distance per stroke, which simply means taking as few strokes as you can to get across the pool. For example, one athlete may want to reduce stride length to maximize propulsion efforts during the course of a lap.

Times are a precise goal that can be controlled. Generally the conditions are going to be good in most big meets. Swimmers are fortunate to be able to control outcomes based on preparation.

There are also energy considerations. Let's say you have 100 units of energy to perform such and such event. Where are you going to place those units? It would not be wise to use up 75 units of your energy in the first 25 yards of a 100-yard race. Then you would not finish strong. But you can't only put in ten percent, because the race would leave you. So each swimmer needs a specific plan on how they will utilize their energy at the highest level possible.

From a psychological perspective, athletes need to know how to conserve units of passion also. How an athlete uses their mental and physical energy needs to be placed appropriately. Based on the competition, they need to be ready with a "Plan B." For example, instead of pacing himself/herself, the athlete may want to risk going out faster against a superior opponent.

We had a swimmer who broke the world record at the NCAA championships in the 200 individual medley. Part of the process of developing him was to bring him through events that were a longer distance than what he would be performing at the end of the year. For instance, I had him racing the 400 individual medley to help build up his endurance for the Olympic games.

Swimming is obviously a very individual sport. How do you incorporate team concepts in such a solo atmosphere?

We're lucky enough to have so many great swimmers here, that they can push each other to be better. I want my athletes to take responsibility for their own progress. Usually once they make the commitment to get better, the winning will follow sooner or later. We've improved every year I've been here.

If you have players that aren't doing so well, it's important that they understand their responsibility to the team. Instead of hanging their heads and getting in a selfish, pitying mode, they need to support their teammates. We had no problem with that this year.

You coached both men's and women's teams to championships. What do you see as the major differences in working with the different genders?

The biggest different I see is that men are internally self-driven, and women are atmosphere/feeling driven. When in doubt, leave men alone. When in doubt with women, make sure they get support, from coaches, parents, or teammates. There are differences by human nature. Men try to fix things and make things right, mold things into the way they want to structure them.

Women want to communicate their feelings more. We had a young lady win the 100-meter butterfly at NCAA's. A lot of getting her prepared was keeping her involved with the team atmosphere. If she had gone to the meet by herself, I don't think we would have seen nearly the same performance.

Women's toughness isn't the same as men's. After the women finish a set I don't tell them, "Okay, we're going to do one more to see what you are made of." Most women wouldn't respond well to that. After they finish a set I might pose the question to them, "What do you think we can do to get better?"

Sometimes when the guys thought they were finished with a workout or a hard set, I'd throw a zinger at them and say, "This one extra set is for toughness." I qualify it by saying, "I know you have given it your best and given it your all, but dig down once more and step up your level."

What traits did your Championship teams at Auburn possess that made them special?

Most teams had substantial character. They followed through on their responsibilities. They had a special bond and really appreciated one another.

They had a lot of faith, represented by their faith in God and in each other. They trusted that their teammates were trying to be the best they could be. Love, faith and character were the foundation of this year's success. Two of our Olympic Gold Medal winners said winning the team championship at AU was more important to them than winning Olympic gold.

The key ingredient for our team was enthusiasm. What I have noticed over the last few years with the teams I've coached, the times when we've been able to pull off our greatest victories in dual meets or conference meets, have only been when enthusiasm is an obvious component of the team atmosphere. We've still won when enthusiasm was missing, but "E" (enthusiasm) has always brought out the best in our

Auburn's team.

How would you describe your coaching style or philosophy?

My style of coaching works more with the ebbs and flows of performance. I don't have a rigid program and say here is the exact routine that we're going to follow. There is no one standard of measure that we are trying to live up to all the time.

Pep talks can be good sometimes, but having role models around is even better. We brought in (Auburn alum and former Olympic champion) Rowdy Gaines to speak, and he visited several practices. Having upperclassmen show younger athletes good work habits is very important.

I like to focus on the process, not the outcome. You have to take athletes through a process of getting better. By slowly moving the bar up, they will usually rise to the occasion. I like to see improvement day to day. I challenge them to take their training to the next level every day with a list of objectives and tests.

Have you ever tried any motivation tactic that backfired?

One time a pep talk didn't go so well is when I brought in a speaker to talk to the guys. He had them fired up and in a frenzy, but it was still 3 hours before we had to compete. The guys had come down by the start of the race. Someone later told me: "I was ready to tear up the world after the team meeting, but at the time we were going to compete, I was tired."

How do you motivate individual athletes and learn what "hot buttons" to push to get the most from their performances?

At the beginning of the year we talk a lot with the swimmers individually to learn what they want from us as coaches. We ask them specifically how they want to be handled before a race.

We had two Olympic gold medal winners, and they couldn't be any more different. One liked us to get in his face and say things like "You're the man." For him, the higher the energy, the better. The other one was introverted and low key and liked to be left alone.

When you do a sweeping motivation thing, you will hit some of them, but others won't respond, or it might hurt their performance.

When you returned to Auburn after a successful career yourself, what steps did you take to rebuild the program that was not living up to past high standards?

One of the first things I wanted to do is restore the pride. There was more of a party atmosphere than anything. I knew we couldn't win a championship the first year, so I immediately started focusing on the long-term future. In 1990, our first goal was to win the Men's SEC by 1994.

On my very first day back I had everyone learn how to do a proper handshake. I told them they had to be firm and look the other person in the eye. Then I had them put a towel around their back and walk like Superman around the pool. I wanted them to know they were representing the best university in the country.

That first year I looked at how well you could improve as an individual. We needed to first re-establish an identity with Auburn swimming. I concentrated on the process not the outcome. I wanted to push them to be better. I avoided rah-rah stuff but made it clear what it would take to accomplish our goals.

What advice would you have for a high school coach to prepare their athletes for the next level of competition?

Be very involved in instilling the ultimate dream. Let their high school experience be an important part of it. Don't let experience hamper their progress. Sometimes, I've seen coaches get extra good results from just pounding the kids in high school during training. Help the athlete get an athletic career plan in place, and realize that it will change as the athlete develops. Set the foundation with proper biomechanics. Put in techniques that will help the athletes maximize distance per stroke.

You've called your coaching philosophy "coaching from the inside out." Can you elaborate more on this? How does that philosophy impact how you interact with and communicate with your athletes?

There are two fronts. From a biomechanical standpoint I like to start with the body alignment (head and spine), then move out to the shoulders, pelvis, knees and elbows and finally to the fingertips.

Second, I've had a slight change in my philosophy. I want to help athletes strive to achieve what they want. I want them to have a firm grasp on what they want to accomplish. My job is to implement a program that will help them get there and hold them accountable.

The athletes need to internally set the direction, then we as coaches and support systems (parents, medical, strength, etc.), must externally help them meet their goals.

- 3 -

J. ROBINSON: CREATING AN UNSHAKEABLE BELIEF SYSTEM

Minnesota wrestling coach J. Robinson has established one of the top wrestling programs in the nation. He is a two time National Wrestling Coaches Association Coach of the Year. He has helped produce 102 All-Americans and has led the team to three national titles.

Do athletes have to be self-motivated to be successful? Can you groom them somewhat?

Coaching, teaching and parenting are all connected. You are trying to transfer life skills and values to someone else. Trying to get someone to change habits at 25 is much more difficult than trying to change a young child. There's a great quote to sum up this principle: "Learn it right, and you will do it right the rest of your life. Learn it wrong, and you will spend the rest of your life trying to get it right."

It's very hard to put motivation into people. Two areas are important in athletics- motivation and skill development. Most good athletes can improve their skills. In most cases, it's very hard to motivate people. You can a lead a horse to water, but you can't make it drink. Many times, coaches will want to win more than athletes do.

How many times have you heard a coach say, "'That kid could really be good if only he would ... show up on time, ... really care about improving his performance, etc."

A psychologist once told me that everything in life is skill development. None of us are born with any specific skills. We all must learn the skills. Most people look at a problem and see the symptoms, not the cause. If you go five layers down and find the root cause, you can solve anything. If you try to fix the symptoms at the first one or two levels, you won't change much. If a coach develops life skills in a kid,

17

you have the foundation to build on.

You like to use motivational sayings. Is that a big part of your coaching? Does that help you maintain the competitive edge at your level?

Bear Bryant once said, "I'm not the smartest guy around. But I can take what other people do and make it work for me." I relate to that. There is a lot of great wisdom out there. As coaches, we try to sum up principles in short sayings that can be remembered.

We're living in an information age where people have so much thrown at them. The key is finding something to stick. I like quotes because they allow me to narrow down a concept, which helps athletes focus on something concrete.

Motivational quotes are part of building that belief system with your athletes the entire time they are in your program. Motivation is a learned skill. If they don't learn how to motivate themselves, you can't get them to do what you want.

Sometimes, as coaches, we develop unrealistic expectations. You can't ask a kid to run before they can walk. Fundamental principles don't change. For example, the same way the Egyptians built the pyramids is the same way you would build them today.

But athletes need the basics in place to succeed later. Those would be dedication, discipline, sacrifice, and most important- a solid work ethic.

Let's say you have a kid come into your program who has dominated in high school, but now they are facing much tougher competition. How do you instill mental toughness in that athlete, especially after defeats or setbacks early on?

First, we have to be realistic with him. He may have never lost in high school, then he gets here and gets beat up pretty bad. We try to talk with our new players alot, especially the freshman. Everyone wants to know that they are like others who have been through similar experiences. So what we do is share a lot of examples of other top guys who have come in and suffered during that initial adjustment period. We tell them you must go through this to get ready for the next level.

We'll tell them, "Hey, the same thing happening to you is what happened to our 4 time All-Americans. They had similar experiences when they were here. They couldn't get any takedowns. They didn't think they were that good anymore."

When you make those comparisons to those great athletes who they may look to as role models, then those newer team members will believe that they are just like everyone else and keep pushing forward.

You have to monitor where they are mentally. We do some things differently then other teams. For example, we dress in the locker room with the kids. We put our coaches lockers next to the freshman lockers. You can see when a kid is up or down or if he is having a hard time adjusting. After a tough practice where he may have been roughed up pretty good you can tell him, "Hey, don't worry about it. The same thing happened to (name several former All-Americans)." It helps you monitor them more closely as opposed to being on the practice field with them, and that's it.

There is an intimacy in wrestling that is different than other sports. We train in the trenches with the guys. I wrestled everyday until I was almost 40, then I couldn't anymore after several knee operations.

The bottom line is that we go into their world instead us trying to bring them into our world. Also, if you have closer contact, especially with the younger guys, you can joke around with them and break down barriers. We have friendly banter with the guys.

We like to keep in close contact with them because they get beat up pretty bad, and they get down on themselves. But if you can catch them right away and talk to them about the big picture, you can give them a time period of how long they have to go through this rough period, which is important. For example we might say, "After three or four months, you will see light at the end of the tunnel."

Now if you don't say anything to them, they will think that this rough period is something that will go on forever. We tell them better times are ahead, and why it will be better in three or four months.

We'll say, "Hey, you are lifting four times a week and increasing your endurance with running." Give them rational reasons they can relate to. "The reason you are here is that your body isn't a machine yet. We are building your endurance. That takes 3 to 4 months to build up. Around January, you will be holding your own." This gives them something to hold on to. One of the most important things in life is hope. It's critical for them to understand that. This helps keep their belief system going. You have to be able to believe in the face of adversity.

One of the biggest challenges for the guys is for them to believe that if they put up with all this added work and sacrifice, there will be a reward for it down the road.

You have to be persistent. What's the difference between being stubborn and focused? People who don't like you call you stubborn. Others who see you working toward a specific goal will call you focused.

It's a two-part system for success. Part 1 is a belief system that is unyielding. You can't compromise. They must keep their belief system in place when they go through shortcomings and down periods. Athletes must be "keepers of the flame." They have to believe when others won't. The second thing is that athletes must enjoy the journey. They have to see the effort they are putting in will pay dividends down the road.

Nothing is more important than an athlete's attitude. It defines everything. The most important question you can ever ask in your life is: "Is the cup half full or half empty?" The world is what it is. How you come at the world is how you perform in life.

What psychological aspects of coaching do you consider most important and why?

Wrestling isn't that different from other sports or life for that matter. The important thing is to channel everything toward developing a belief system. Succeeding in athletics comes down to believing that you can do it. From a psychological standpoint, anything you can do to build a belief system in your athletes is key.

Example: Coaches talk to kids about what they need to do - get psyched up, etc, but they don't really tell them specifically what to do. Everyone has a belief system, and as you grow older that system grows. The more you accomplish, the more you believe you can accomplish. It's a continual process. The core of any belief system can be summed up by the phrase "preparation changes expectations."

The more you prepare, the more you believe you will do well. This doesn't just apply to athletics. Most of us already know the answers. One of our assistant coaches will tell our athletes, "We are giving you the answers to the test ahead of time. The question becomes, are you going to listen and prepare?"

At my summer wrestling camp, I will ask the kids if they had ever taken a test and not studied. What are your expectations? Most will say that they hope to get a C.

Then, I will ask if they ever had a class they really liked and studied more than anyone else. You did everything the teacher asked to do in advance. Now, what were your expectations? Most will say an A. So athletes know what they need to do. The question becomes, will they do what it takes?

Since you mentioned having such a close relationship with your players, does that mean you don't need to give them pep talks. Is there a time when you really need to pump them up?

Different matches require different things. Some people peak with certain things. You have to understand what is going on during the big matches. What you want to do is re-affirm the things that you have already done. You reinforce concepts like "preparation changes expectation." This is what we did in practice. This is why we did it. This is how it's going to help you. Everyone is going through their pre-match mindset where they may have fears and doubts. As coaches, we need to quell those doubts and fears. We talk to the team with definitive reasoning.

For example, when we won the nationals in 2001, we had a three-day training cycle during the season. Normally, most teams have two day. First day fresh, second day tired, third day they were really beat up. But all during the year we told them on the third day - this is our day. This is the NCAA tournament. This is when everyone else is tired and wants to go home. This is what we are training for now. So before the finals in 2001, we had a team meeting. It wasn't a really rah-rah deal, but it was a reminder of what the team had done all year. We reminded them of the price they paid to get here. We told them, "This is what we have worked for. This is our day." Everyone else was probably telling their guys the same thing. But we told our guys, "This is your day because you did 1, 2, 3." That makes a difference. You've invested so much in this. The more you invest, the more you believe.

Talk about your mentors and some of the coaches who have influenced you and how your coaching philosophy impacts what you do.

Life is like a journey. As coaches, we take bits and pieces from different people. Some of the most influential guys were my high school and college coaches. I learned from them that I need to have a philosophy of what coaching is about. Most coaches know how to teach different moves, but they don't have a core philosophy behind it.

A lot of us don't have the fundamentals in place, so we bounce all around and do what is trendy or cool at the time. But that turns the pyramid upside down. Our philosophy is to be aggressive and dominant and always go forward. That is our mission statement. Then you build everything from there. This allows us to have a clear focus, "Are we going to try this technique. If it doesn't fit into our philosophy, no."

"Are we going to hang around the edge of the mat? No, because it contradicts our philosophy of always pushing forward. So we never teach anything about that."

Once you have established a core philosophy, you can build everything around it. You focus on what's really important and discard the rest. It helps all the kids because they understand what you are trying to do. So many times, coaches will shift their focus depending on what's going on today. You want to have a set of fundamentals in place that will work for everyone.

Can you discuss goal setting within your coaching philosophy?

I read an article once on business management that said you have to control what you can control and forget the rest. For example, IBM can't control if they are the top corporation in the world. I can't control whether we win the NCAA. You can control your level of customer service; you can control being aggressive and dominant and having fun. If I tell you to do these 3 things every day, you could. Those are daily goals. If you can maximize those 3 things every day, the rest will take care of itself.

So our 3 team goals are to: 1) Be aggressive. 2) Dominate. 3) Have fun.

If I had to add a fourth goal, it would be to improve every day. You can control whether you improve on a skill or not. If you get better, you will win more.

Saying you want to win more is too vague and intangible. You can't control it. Every kid can control whether they get better than they were the day before.

For example, I might ask a kid, "'Can you improve 1 percent tomorrow? Would that be asking too much?'"

If a kid can improve just 1 percent a day - in 3 months they will be 90 percent better than they are now. If you are 90 percent better in 3 months, are you going to win more? You bet. Now, you have a road map to get where you want that is within your capacity to control.

In goal setting, you need to set goals that are within your reach. It's back to the pyramid. If you build the base, everything will come after it. The base is responsibility, accountability, hard work, discipline, sacrifice and dedication. Those are the core principles of being a good athlete.

But if you can't get to practice on time, you won't be in proper shape. If you don't do your academics, you won't be eligible. Or if you have a bad temper and you can't get along with your teammates, you won't succeed.

What are your views on rules and discipline? What do you do when a kid gets out of line?

You try to talk with them first, but sometimes you have to punish them. If a kid has it in his mind that he doesn't want to change his behaviors, you will spend a lot of time trying to get someone to turn around.

With some kids, you get to the point where you ask, "'Is this good or bad for the team as a whole?" Sometimes, there are kids you just can't save. There is the old 90 -10 philosophy. If you keep making allowances for the bad ten percent, then the other kids see it, and they want to know why. If it's because the kid is a really great athlete, all of the sudden you have a different set of rules for star athletes. That impacts the team negatively.

Realistically, we'll work with kids up to a certain point. But when an athlete's behavior crosses a line, you have to stop it because it affects the entire team through poor example. It doesn't take much to undo all the good work that you have accomplished.

We don't have many rules. If you are training hard, most of the stuff takes care of itself. If you are getting up at 6 AM to train, the odds are you will get in bed at a decent hour to prepare yourself for that.

The real key to everything is to answer the question, "Where do you want to go?" Once you know the answer to that question, it dictates all your other behaviors.

I ask young kids at my camps, "If you want to be the greatest lawyer in the United States, where would you go to school?" Most everyone will say Harvard. So people know what to do. It's not a question of not knowing what to do. The key in life is not knowledge. The key is action. Doing what you need to do. Life is about making the right choices. No choice is a choice. Taking action means doing the things you don't want to do.

What type of punishments would you dole out?

It depends on whom you are dealing with and what the specific infraction was. If it's a group problem, you deal with it as a team problem.

Example: Let's say a kid comes to my camp and he takes something from another kid. Now, no one is going to turn in this kid or "rat them out." However, if I get the whole group up to run an hour early because of one kid's actions, there is a good chance the stolen item might be returned.

Example 2: Now if it's a kid who can't get to practice on time, you make them come back at a time that is very inconvenient for them. Maybe he wants to go out with his girlfriend on Friday night. Instead, you have him come back at 9 PM for extra practice. Now you are infringing upon his time. The message is- there are consequences to your actions. You have to get the message into them that they are responsible for their actions, and they will be held accountable for them.

Regarding academics, we demand they put in extra time in study hall depending on where their grade point average is. If it's such and such, then you must put in an extra 10 hours and so on. I tell them, "I'm not the bad guy. You are doing this to yourself because of your lack of action or discipline." I try to bring the consequence back on them. If there is no consequence, behavior won't change. There is no reason to change. If you do improper behavior A, then you get consequence A. But you don't dwell on the punishment. You punish them, then move on. Now, let's get back to moving forward again.

- 4 -

FRANK LENTI: MAXIMUM MOTIVATION FOR THE HIGH SCHOOL ATHLETE

Mt. Carmel (IL) high school football coach Frank Lenti's teams have played for 11 state titles and won 9. They were named the Illinois team of the decade in the 1990s.

Discuss how you motivate your team.

I think first of motivating the individual, then the team. We try to appeal to their individual pride, "What do you want to be remembered for?" There is no sense being part of our program unless you are going to contribute in some way. This doesn't mean being a starter or a star, but that you get something back from your investment. We tell kids, "When you spend a dollar, you don't get much back. Invest a dollar and you'll see some return on that investment." We want the kids to invest their time in their education and athletic career. This way they are assured of getting something back from their efforts.

We have a program called the 4 E's. In everything they do while in our program we stress the following: Great Effort. Great Execution. Great Endurance. Great Enthusiasm. These principles apply to school, social and athletic situations.

Giving great effort and endurance speaks for themselves. Execution means doing the fundamentals well, whether it is in football or in school.

Regarding enthusiasm, we have a slogan painted on the locker room wall-"Fun is doing something well." School is fun when you are getting A's and B's, yet it's a real pain when you get D's and F's. It's fun if a kid does well in practice. We are always talking to kids about raising their standards.

27

Another saying we tell kids is: "If it is to be, it's up to me." We want the kids to take responsibility for their success. The key motivating factor for the kids comes from Zig Ziglar, "You can get anything in this world you want if you are willing to help enough other people get what they want."

The reason we have been so successful at Mt. Carmel is that our coaching staff has helped the guys get what they want- which is to be a success as people, students and athletes.

Could you describe some motivational approaches you have used with individual athletes or the entire team that weren't successful?

The one thing we have done over the years wrong is to get the kids too high for a certain game. We don't want them so excited that they lose track of their fundamentals and assignments. When the emotional high wears off after the first few moments of the game, they sometimes get into a fog. Sometimes, we got the guys too emotionally invested in one particular game. The remedy for this is to eliminate any "red letter" or one certain "game of the year" mentality. We want our kids thinking that the most important game of the year is the next one, regardless of the opponent. This falls in line with another principle we try to teach, "consistency is more important than greatness."

It's no good for the team if a guy is great for a quarter and then falls asleep at the switch for the rest of the game. I'd rather see a kid play good and consistent all game long. This way we know we can count on him.

Do you work with kids from broken families? Is there any advice you can give to coaches who are in a similar situation?

The number one issue here is building trust. It's a two-way street. Later on, some of these kids will come back and say that we were like the father they never had. When they need a male figure to talk to, we as coaches have to be available.

You might have to invest a little more time in these types of kids.

Whether it's a one to one in the coach's office, in the classroom, or on the field before or after practice, coaches need to be available. You have to find out some personal information about what is going on in their lives.

Example: Two days a week we like to bring in our offensive kids early to watch film before school. We had a two year starter who could not come in early because he had to take his younger brother to school because his grandmother left for work already, and there were no mom and dad around. If I make things difficult for that kid, we'll end up losing him. Since he has a tough home situation, we'll be flexible and have him watch tape with the defense at another time. It's now up to him to make it to the lunch-time film session. There is always give and take in these situations.

What is your general approach to team discipline? Do you believe in a strict adherence to rules? Do high school athletes need more rules than a college athlete?

Our philosophy in this area is really simple. The heart and soul of the rule I got from Coach Lou Holtz. We tell them to "do what's right." We break that down into doing what's right as a person, as a student and as an athlete. That's the order of importance for us.

Example: Let's say one of the players is hanging out at the mall with a Mount Carmel Letterman's jacket on and he acts like a nitwit. Guess what? Eventually we're going to find out about that. I'd much rather get a call that says a player held the door open for some nice little old lady rather than finding out he tried to run her over.

I tell our kids that they are leaders of the school. They help set the tempo each year by their actions. I don't want to have a teacher come into my office and tell me, "one of your players was misbehaving." They won't say Johnny so and so was misbehaving, they'll say one of the football players was misbehaving.

Because of the success of the program, our players are highly visible. We tell them it does us no good for Mount Carmel to win state championships if we can't get you into college when the time comes. Again we talk about developing the leadership roles. (Mt. Carmel has put kids into the Ivy League schools, the service academies and all levels of NCAA).

Is there anything specific about your leadership training?

We try to get kids to understand that they are ultimately responsible for their success and their failures. We tell them, "the pain of discipline is never as bad or difficult as the pain of regret." If you have the discipline to do the right things all the time, then you will have few regrets in life. Another thing we teach about is choices. The big thing we want our kids to understand is that if they make poor choices, then they will not get to choose the consequences.

Do you want them to see that the consequences will be forced upon then?

Right. Someone else is going to choose the consequences for them. For example, if you choose to be late for school or you choose to misbehave in class, you're going to end up with a detention. You don't get to choose when to serve that detention. It may make you miss something very important. We also talk about forcing the kids to measure up. Every decision you make is going to affect you, your family, and your teammates either positively or negatively. If you make the decision to be a goof in class and you get a detention, that doesn't just affect you. It now affects everyone in practice because you can't be there to do your fair share, and you can't be there to get better.

Does that message usually resonate with the kids you work with by telling them, "Look it's not just you that suffers, but also everybody else when you make a bad choice?"

I learned something very valuable from Coach Lou Holtz - "the people that you hang around with are either going to bring you up or tear you down." So I think my players understand what we're communicating.

Do you do anything differently from year to year with regards to team building, or do you just stick with the same plan?

Quite honestly, it's pretty much a basic plan that we modify and tweak a bit based on the personalities of the kids you're dealing with. Sometimes you have a group that's highly motivated. Those kids don't have to be leaned on that much. With a program like ours, with the success that we've have, the thing that we have to be concerned with is that the kids don't take that success for granted. Since 1995 we've only missed the championship two times. I firmly believe that when we didn't win it was because we had some players who were "me" guys and not "we" guys. Part of our philosophy is, if you want to be a success, it has to be a "we" thing not a "me" thing.

I have an old book written by Knute Rockne in 1925 that has some timeless wisdom. One of the great quotes from this book was the following: "I don't play my 11 best, but my best 11." In other words, he was saying it's not the 11 best individual athletes, but the 11 who best fit together that really counts.

Let's break it down- how do you get these guys that are only out for themselves to buy into the whole team concept?

I read a lot about other successful coaches. Guys like John Wooden have taught me that the best friend you have is the bench. You have to be willing to give the bench a try in the short term to give your program a chance to be more successful in the long run.

One of the things we address is chemistry. How do guys fit in with the team and group atmosphere? Here's an example I like to use. We might have some hot shot sophomore running back come up to the varsity team, and I'll have people ask me why isn't he playing more? He was great as a freshman and I'll tell them that he does not fit in yet. He still thinks it's about himself. When he learns that it's "we" thing rather than a "me" thing, then he will get on the field.

Is this like paying your dues first, or is it a little more involved than that?

I don't think of it as paying your dues. I think in terms of you've just got to put your time in and demonstrate that you are willing to invest in the team. Being willing to make the small sacrifices that are going to give the team an opportunity to be a success.

One thing I like to tell people is that with all the success we've had, kids have got to realize we know what to do to get them to the end of the road, and we're going to do it together.

I like to tell the story about (Tampa Bay Buccaneer All-Pro) Simeon Rice. He didn't start until his senior year. He spent most of his junior year on the bench for his poor attitude.

One of our team building goals is to find a way for kids to participate-either in games or practice. Don't discount participation in practice because kids are going to be motivated if they see themselves getting better.

If a kid is on your practice field and he spends three fourths of his time watching someone else, what motivates him to get better? If you get kids involved in practice and they can participate, now they realize that they'll eventually get a chance to participate in the game. One of the things we tell our kids all the time to motivate them is that the game of football is not just about talent. A guy can have great talent, but if he won't do what we want him to do, he's not any better than a kid who can't do what we want.

In the nineties we were known as the team of the decade. In all those successes we've never had a player be the leading passer, rusher, receiver, etc.

How can you have not had any players hold a "leading" position after winning all those state titles? Is that because you've stressed the team concept over the individual?

Exactly. We're going to play a lot of players- period. What motivates our kids to get better is knowing that if they work hard and are aware of their assignments, then eventually they are going to get an opportunity to participate.

We've never had anyone be the all area leading anything in those categories. At one time we had eight players and one graduate assistant playing at the University of Illinois at the same time. Our goal is to have the kids be ready to graduate from Mount Carmel and go onto college. Playing football is part of the icing on the cake.

You have spoken about the common traits of the championship team- is there something to add on the subject?

The old line, "hard work works." If you're not willing to work hard, what are your opportunities for being a success? It's the old theory that everybody's going to work hard because they want to be a success, but what are you going to do to "out work the competition?"

Can you talk somewhat on your physical and off-season training?

As far as physical training, we don't even start our off-season weight training until the beginning of March every year. We give them a couple of months off. Some people start before Christmas vacation- that's not our plan.

Is it counter productive to start right after the season ends?

When it comes time for football, I want the kids excited and ready to play football. When it comes time to be in the weight room, I want them to want to be there.

We want our kids investing their time wisely. A lot of kids start lifting in December and January. By the end of the school year, they are tired of being in the weight room. That's why we prefer they wait until the spring to start hitting the weights.

What else do you do in the off-season to make sure they are participating in your weight program? Do you go back to investing the time to make the success?

The number one reason for weight lifting for us is injury prevention. We point out examples of guys who have been injured over the years because they didn't lift in the off-season. The players not making an investment for me- they are making an investment for themselves and the team. You don't do this because I want you to do it. You do it because you want to be a success. When it comes to the summer and the fall, it's your team. How do you want your chapter of Mount Carmel football history to read? The more you put into it, the more you're going to get out of it.

- 5 -

SUZANNE YOCULAN: VISUALIZING SUCCESS LEADS TO 9 NATIONAL TITLES

Former University of Georgia Gymnastics Coach Suzanne Yoculan produced 9 national championship teams and 33 individual NCAA champions.

You've coached 9 national championship teams. What common traits did your NCAA championship teams possess that helped them become champions?

There were different traits on the team that has never won a championship and the recent teams that have won four in a row. That first championship was won with enthusiasm and a kind of blind "go for it all" attitude.

If I had to pick one common trait it would be the picture. When I first arrived at Georgia in 1984, I always said to the team that our picture is to win a national championship. From the very beginning, I talked to them about what that would look like from a visual standpoint. I would ask them, "What do you see when I talk about winning a national championship?" They would say, running down the runway, sticking a vault, holding up a trophy, and various other things. Instead of incremental step goals like making the NCAA regionals, I set a big picture goal of winning it all from the start. The common trait is that all the teams have shared that vision or picture.

What are mental training techniques you've taught the team that you feel are most important?

Believing you can be successful is first- whatever that picture of success looks like to you. We do a lot of imagery. One year we were having problems on balance beam, so we had little wooden balance beams made of Popsicle sticks. I asked the team to put the sticks on dressers in their dorm room and every time they looked at them to shut their eyes and do their imagery of a perfect beam routine.

We encourage imagery before the balance beam routine in practice and during competitions. We use a stopwatch and time them to make sure the length of their visualization is the actual time of their routine. If their routine is a minute and ten, but their imagery only lasts 30 seconds, we teach them to slow down mentally. This helps them if they feel nervous or anxious in competition. We do more of this with the freshman.

I'm a big believer in "what works for you." We have some very high-level athletes who have had a lot of success prior to coming here. I don't try to change things. For example, if an athlete has had great success in the past on the beam without using imagery, we won't ask them to do any.

If someone has a competitive performance that is lower than what they are doing in practice, it has everything to do with pressure and fear of failure.

What do you say, or how do you coach during or after a competition with an athlete who is struggling with handling competitive pressure?

One of the first things I do is to make sure she is not in "overload" mode. Many coaches coach too much. They give too much information- too many cues. It's a mistake when you tell an athlete five things at once, instead of one. I want to make sure she is not getting too much information from too many people. I may have to address this with the other coaches. I'll then have the athletes focus on two cues. One is a technical cue that they write on their left hand (which might be a phrase like head back or arms straight). This technical cue can change depending on what event they are doing. On beam, it could be chin up. On their right hand, I have them write an emotional cue. One of our five-time national champions will write "ferocious." She likes to think of herself as ferocious or fierce.

Our regular season is a time where we can afford to lose a few meets and still quality for the post-season, which reinforces my view of looking at the process and not over-reacting to mistakes or wins or losses.

Besides getting talented gymnasts into your program, what are the key factors to maintaining such a consistent level of success over twenty plus seasons?

Knowing what you stand for. No team, sports or business, can have three decades of success without knowing what they stand for and making it very clear to the people on the team. The mission needs to be very clear. Everyone needs to share the vision and the strategies of how we get there. It comes down to what and how we prioritize as a team.

One of the things our program has spent a lot of time on is communication. Even before the concept was really popular 20 years ago, I've believed in having open communication at team meetings and building team unity. We stand for respect. Years ago, I couldn't put it into words, but there has always been a level of respect that has permeated our program- from team member to team member, between coaches, and between coaches and athletes. Respect is something that is earned, and we spend a lot of time developing these type of relationship with athletes. We've never had another athlete transfer to compete another school in my entire tenure. It's not a self-promotion thing. It's a program credential. We prioritize the respect level and well-being of the athlete.

Gymnastics requires great mental toughness. How do you help gymnasts deal with failure inherent in the sport?

We don't deal with failure because we don't believe in any failure. There isn't failure- only partial success. We emphasize that there is something to be learned in the process. One of the reasons I'm not afraid to say, "we're going to win the national title" and then finish third- I don't consider that failure. Too many people don't set high expectations because they are afraid of failure, so they lower the bar.

When coaching injured athletes, what are the best ways to communicate with them during the rehab process? How do you make sure they are mentally ready to compete once they have recovered?

One of the things we have always made sure of is that we don't spend more time and energy on the top scorers than the rest of the team, whether they are injured or healthy.

Injuries are such a common part of the sport, and we talk about how to prepare for them before the athlete has to deal with them. We always stress that they need to measure their success over the long haul of their careers- not just at any one point where they may be struggling. If they have a major injury, we'll give them a more pronounced role on the team. It may be developing music videos for teammates or helping the assistant coaches with different tasks. We never remove them off to another area. Our training and rehabilitation center is right together in the gym. We have our cardio equipment in a place where the person working on rehab can see everyone else while they are training.

Have you ever used some motivational tactics with individual athletes or the entire team that weren't entirely successful?

Early in my career I used to have too many rules. This can backfire because athletes can get confused about too long a list of do's and don'ts. Another error was looking to lead the team the same way I did in the past with different personalities. It's important to be spontaneous and read the team as to where they are emotionally at any given time.

In the 1990s, I used to be a believer that everyone had to compete for her spot in the line-up. If someone made a mistake, then she were out the next week and had to earn her way back in. I thought that was good motivation -"stay on the equipment or you are out." Really, that was negative motivation. It didn't work well at all. It just added to the pressure, so instead of the athlete being able to go into a competition relaxed and ready to perform, they knew if they didn't stay on the beam or bars, they were out the next week. That was a motivational trick that didn't work out as I intended.

How do you recommend coaches handle the psyches of the more emotionally fragile gymnasts?

We've had individual team meetings with the girls since 1998 as part of our 20 hours of practice. They didn't enjoy them at first, but later on they become one of the things they most look forward to during the season. It's important to be available to your athletes and I've tried to have an open door policy and be a resource to them.

Motivational movies- how do you put those together, and when is the best time of year to get the most impact?

We mainly do motivational movies as we get ready for the SEC and national meets. I'm totally spontaneous. I have to get a feel for what the team needs at that time before I can do anything.

For example, after the 2007 season we lost 2 All-American seniors who competed in all 4 events. We lost 8 of 24 routines from our line-up due to injuries. One happened just days before we left for the nationals. The mood of the team was down. I decided that I wanted the focus or theme of the national championships to be on "fight." I went to the football coach's office because they have lots of motivational videos and asked if they had a video that emphasized fighting. I used a Muhammad Ali movie video whose message was "when you think you are down, you're not. When everyone counts you out, including the fans who think you don't stand a chance, you can fight through the adversity." That was the message of the movie.

So we used clips from that movie and inserted some of our own video. It starts out with scenes where Ali is getting beat up, then we showed some of our early season struggles where we looked like we were beaten and down for the count. Then we showed examples where our team was tenacious and fought back. It ends with the scene where Ali comes out and runs through the fans and wins the big fight at the end. The team was so excited after watching the video that they were like, "yea, let's go kick some butt."

Nationals are a two-day event. Fight was the theme for the first day, because you have to qualify the first day to advance to the second round. We won the first day, which really helped the team's confidence. Focus was the theme of the second day. I wanted them to narrow their focus. Then I had the team watch clips from the movie "The Last Samurai" which is all about focus and realizing that without focus you can't succeed. The message resonates through the whole movie. Then I had parents of the athletes wear Samurai headbands at the meet. The girls had their focus words on their hands. I pulled off the bedding in the hotel room and had them make a tunnel with the quilt. I had the team who was competing on the beam do their routines inside the tunnel to narrow their focus and visualize that there was a wall on either side of them.

We never missed a beat. After making a mistake, we remained focused. I told the team right before the final day that we didn't need to be perfect. Our main rival that year was Florida and they had beaten us during the regular season and SEC tournament, so they were the big favorite. I said, "Instead of worrying about being perfect, we need to not become distracted after making mistakes- just focus on what you are doing and not on your teammates or the other team." The rival coach did just the opposite. She told her team that they needed to be perfect to win the tournament, which was the wrong thing to say (before such a high pressure event.) I told our team the way we react to mistakes would make the difference on how well we performed.

In the first half of the meet, we had about the same number of mistakes. When their team was on a bye (not on the floor competing), they were watching us. When we were on a bye, we had the door shut to our locker room and were dancing. We didn't get concerned about what the other team was doing.

Gymnastics is a very individual sport that operates within the framework of a team. What are some of the challenges that must be overcome to build team unity in such an environment?

Our team emphasizes team cohesiveness so much. There is not one unkind word or bad feeling between the girls. Also, there is nothing we are afraid to discuss as a team. So many teams struggle with divisions.

It can be between seniors and freshman, between black and white, gay and straight athletes. A lot of coaches don't want to talk about these issues and want to bury them under the rug. They cause divisiveness. One of the issues we have had to deal with is drinking and non-drinking. We have nothing sacred. Our policy is that if an issue involves the respect level and cohesiveness of the team, the issue has to be put out on the table and discussed. Certainly, there are private matters that some of the girls don't want to share. But if it's an issue that is causing any kind of tension, it impacts the team as a whole. Once you lose that lack of trust and love between teammates, when you get out on the field or gym, you just don't play as hard. But if you have a great relationship with your teammates, you'll eat dirt for them if it comes down to it. We keep jealousy and animosity to an absolute minimum. It's hard to implement however.

Do you do anything differently for preparing to compete at the nationals than you would during regular season meets?

We approach the regular season as part of a process. We never put emphasis on results. Some coaches may have a goal to hit 24 out of 24 routines. That's a result. If you do everything right, you will hit 24 out of 24. We try not to talk about results in any of our conversations. Every single week, I remind them that it's not important what we do Friday and Saturday at the competition. It's what we do on Monday after we have the results that counts. For example, let's say we won a match by a sizeable margin. Are we going to get our heads too big? We've been ranked pre-season number one 19 times, so it's very important not to get caught up in the ranking thing. On Monday, we review the results, what our current emotional state is, and where were our problem areas are and what we need to do to work on those.

What are your thoughts on post-game team meetings?

I never talk to the team immediately after a competition. I wait until Monday. After a match, I just tell them "Circle up and Go Dawgs!" Then we leave. If a freshman had a particularly difficult meet, I may call them and have them meet me in the office the next morning. I like to review what happened and process it on my own before addressing the team Monday. This is a relatively recent change in my coaching philosophy. I remember screaming during post competition meetings in the 80s and early 90s. The way I see it is if they do well and they are happy about it, what I say won't really matter anyway because they are ready to celebrate. If they did poorly and they are upset, they will tune me out. This change was preceded by a conversation I saw on my daughter's college soccer team. After a loss, the coach would have them all sitting on a field discussing what just happened in 30-degree weather, and I'm thinking to myself, "very few of the players are really listening to the coach right now."

What really helped me become a better coach was watching my children's athletic careers as they progressed through the college level. Both were great athletes who were held back from reaching their full potential by their mental game. Seeing things from my children's perspective while watching other coaches helped me tremendously. I used to be so reactive and even throw my shoes after a meet. Now, I just collect all the information I can and think about what we need to do next. It's easier to make decisions that way.

What are some coaching philosophies that have changed over the years?

I learned all this from making lots of mistakes early in my career. I would see things strictly in black and white and be one of those "my way or the highway" coaches. I've learned to listen to the athletes and be more responsive - to include them in as many aspects of our program as possible, from how they do conditioning to when they practice. Sometimes, I'll even ask them to decide who will be in the line-up. They will sit in a room for hours and come back and tell me that it's too hard and they don't want to do it. Even though I've only done that a few times in 27 years of coaching, it was a good motivational tactic because they saw how difficult it is to decide (who gets to perform).

If you were talking to a young gymnastics coach, what advice would you tell them on what it takes to achieve greatness in their sport?

First and foremost is to listen to their athletes. Bring the athletes in to the decision-making process as much as possible. Make them be examples of whatever your program is going to stand for. Have them help determine what those standards are. It's similar to a mission statement with a company. One key to success is to have the employees involved in writing that mission statement. It's the same thing with your athletes - involve them because when everyone embraces the decisions, they feel more responsible about following through on the priorities set by the team. I've told my successor to make sure he continues the individual and team meetings we have every Monday for 90 minutes. It's important not to have meetings that react to problems. Instead, have a planned agenda of what you are going to discuss that day. Each individual within the team needs different things to be successful, so I focus on the individual first and team second. This is the key to team cohesiveness.

- 6 -

MARK JOHNSON: ENHANCING COMPETITIVENESS & DEVELOPING TEAM LEADERS

Johnson has led the University of Wisconsin Women's Ice Hockey Team to 4 NCAA titles. He played on the 1980 "Miracle on Ice" Olympic Hockey Team, which beat the Soviet Union and Finland to capture the gold medal.

Do you prepare the team any differently during the play-offs as opposed to the regular season? Do you keep pushing the team hard or back off a little bit?

With the magnitude of the play-offs, everything goes up a couple of notches in regards to intensity. We want to create an atmosphere where the athlete has fun and works hard. I want all my athletes excited about the hour and a half we will spend together at the rink. With that type of attitude, I have a chance to make them better players.

As the season winds down, practice times will get shorter. Instead of going an hour and 15 minutes, we may only go 50 minutes. The same attitude and work habits should be in place, so we'll just tweak things a little bit at play-off time. What your body gets used to doing (conditioning wise), it wants to continue doing. By shortening practice, you keep the players physically fresh, but just as important, you keep them fresh mentally as well. Just like if someone is training for an ironman race, that last two weeks they will taper off a little bit, but they will still train.

You've coached both men and women. Could you describe some ways in which men and women respond differently from a motivational standpoint?

With women, their communication skills are a little more in depth. For example, they may want a greater explanation of why we are doing something - whether it's a system type drill or conditioning drill. Instead of just diagramming it and demonstrating it, they want you to explain why they are going to do it. That ties in with the motivational, because now they understand why they are doing a particular drill, and they see how it fits into the bigger picture of our success.

Do you do any drills in practice specifically to enhance your team's mental toughness?

Not specifically. We try to do some competitive and conditioning drills that challenge them. I want to create an environment and culture that kids will have an opportunity to be successful. A key part of that is having good work habits. Their vision of what hard work is may be different from our staff.

If we aren't seeing them working hard, we will put the team in certain competitive situations that will challenge them. A by-product of these competitive situations will be enhanced mental toughness. When they are tired and aren't feeling like practicing because they have just gone through 6-week exams, you want to build in daily work habits that will benefit the team over the course of the season.

If I need to pick up the intensity in practice, I will introduce some type of small game situations. At different points of the season, I recognize that players get tired of doing drills. The energy level picks up fast in a game situation due to their competitive nature.

Could you give a specific example?

You might create a 3 on 2 game. Have 2 lines, and alternate the 3. The red line will come out with 3 players and go against two from the white line. When I blow the whistle after 40 or 50 seconds, it reverses. We go against each other like this for 8 or 9 minutes. Then we might create an overtime situation. The goal is to get the competitive nature going. If the players aren't into a practice because their minds are somewhere else, you do one of these drills and pretty soon it mentally clicks in, and you get them focused so that we can get something out of the practice. At this point, all I have to do is sit back and watch.

Is there any benefit to a pep talk speech before a game?

Pep talks are good when they are kept short and to the point. Don't get too long-winded. If you have a competitive group, they understand the situation. I like to tell some kinds of stories. I will either try to incorporate some type of humor or hit on something that ties in with that particular moment before a game.

How do you come up with those?

One is my own personal history and experiences. The other is from reading about other athletes and the hardships they have faced and how they got through it- life lessons, basically. Most of the time, the talks are unrelated to hockey.

Do you do any pre-season activities to help bring the team together?

Once they are back on campus and finished with academic and compliance meetings, we like to do something together. We've done the ropes courses several different times. We've done curling, golfing, and other group activities, which give the freshman an opportunity to get to know the upperclassmen in a non-pressure, non-threatening type situation. The team gets to know each other in a relaxed setting.

It's also an opportunity for us as coaches to observe and visualize who the team leaders might be. Who are the kids that step forward when there is confusion or something needs to get done? These types of events are great for watching and seeing possible future leaders.

What are the expectations of your team leaders?

This past season we sat down with all of our seniors, and we talked about leadership. We went over the areas we thought it was important to have solid leadership. We wanted to equip them with tools they needed before the season began that would help bring the team together. You can't just put a captain or an assistant captain title on someone's jersey and then tell the player, "Okay, go be a leader." There are many books on the subject, but one of our jobs is to educate players on what it really means to be a leader. If we can do that as coaches, we don't have to deal with some of the small issues that come up over the course of a year. The goal is that when the season progresses they will take care of more issues themselves, and you basically turn the team over to the players.

We tell our seniors that this is their last hurrah, their last chance to play at a very high level of competitive hockey within a team atmosphere. We challenge them by asking, "What do you want to do with this season?"

When you equip them with the tools to be good leaders, as the season progresses they are more and more responsible for the team's identity, and it becomes their team. It's not about our coaches- it becomes more about what they are going to do among themselves to come together as a group.

Are there any specific leader tools you want to convey to the team?

Before this past season, I gave my two assistants and myself the platform to address the team for 8 to 10 minutes on what each of us thought was important to be a team leader. We then asked the team to give some input as well.

Each year is different. For this next group, we'll have a much quieter and laid-back team than we had this past season. So we'll focus on areas that will address this team's personality from a leadership standpoint.

What's great about college hockey is that each group goes through different stages every season. From forming, storming and norming to performing, they have to walk through the season like they go through adolescence. You make them aware in advance that the team is going to go through these stages- especially storming, and let them know it's ok as long as the team comes out of it understanding certain roles and responsibilities are going to have to take shape to actually become a team.

You played for Herb Brooks and were part of one of the greatest moments in sports history (the 1980 United States Gold Medal winning Olympic hockey team). What ideas/concepts did you take from Coach Brooks or lessons/advice you took away from any other coaching mentors?

As a young coach years ago, I was trying to form my identity and coaching philosophy. You back track on your playing experience and say to yourself, "Okay, what did Herb Brooks do that I thought was good? What did my Dad do that worked well?" You then take bits and pieces of experiences you had as a player and mold that into what you really believe in and how you want to be perceived as a coach.

My Dad had the biggest influence on creating a team culture where the kids can have fun coming to the rink and work on forming good habits. Success will be a by-product of that.

The number one thing to bringing a player up to their potential is making it fun when they come to the rink. It's like any job- if you enjoy what you do, it's easy to get up in the morning and go to work.

What common traits did the past two Wisconsin NCAA championship teams possess that helped them become champions?

Similarities would include the ability to be consistent over the course of an entire season in their work habits. They both played up to their potential, game in and game out. It's a long season starting in September and not finishing until the end of March. Our theme was to try to get better each game. Over a 5 or 6-month period, we should be a much better team than when we started.

Were there any unique challenges in trying to repeat as champions from a motivational standpoint? How did you address these with the team?

There will always be challenges after you win something when you get the recognition and press and media. It's human nature to feel good about yourself. As that group disassembled in the spring after finals and headed back home, we had a team meeting and talked with the group coming back. We tried to get them to understand what the summer needed to look like if they wanted to come in the following year and have another great season. I told them there were no guarantees, and they needed to take care of business as far as conditioning and off ice things to have the opportunity to be successful.

For the junior class, it would be their last hurrah. The thing I was most impressed with this group is that when they came back from the summer, they had prepared themselves for the season. They have individualized off-season workouts. When they come back to school, we test them. Talk is cheap. You can tell me what you did, but testing lets us know if you followed through or not. The better they do of preparing, the better chance they have to be successful. If they think they can prepare by the time they get back to school, it's too late.

- 7 -

URBAN MEYER: QUICKLY CHANGING THE TEAM CULTURE

Ohio State University Head Football Coach Urban Meyer formerly led the University of Florida to 2 National Titles in six seasons. Prior to that, he led the University of Utah to an undefeated season in his second year.

Urban Meyer's list of motivational tactics may be more intricate than his playbook. The Florida Gator coach uses countless methods to encourage, energize and entice players to improve every aspect of their lives. He has the Champions Club, Circle of Life and Mat Drills, Hell Lifts, Rookie Stripes and The Pit.

When Meyer took over as Florida head coach last year, his first goal was to familiarize himself with players and see if they were "living right." He hosted several cookouts and began dropping by players' apartments and dormitories with little or no warning.

Assistants put together detailed lists about their players, something Meyer had learned how to do under legendary Ohio State coach Earle Bruce. Meyer wanted his coaches to know names of girlfriends, friends, parents, majors, grade point averages, projected graduation dates and important phone numbers.

"You get so tight with your players that they can't let you down," associate head coach Doc Holliday says. "They don't want to let you down. They're going to play for you. That's why we do all we do."

The hands-on approach allowed Meyer to learn a lot about his players early.

He even broke them down into three academic categories- scarlet, red and gold. Scarlet players are monitored constantly to make sure they're

attending classes. This player needs to re-examine his priorities.
Red players are watched, but not as closely. This player needs some
supervision.

Gold players aren't checked and don't have to attend study hall. A gold
player has proven himself unlikely to skip class, fail a test, or get arrested.

For a player who isn't holding up their end of the bargain, Meyer gets
creative in his punishments. For example, if a running back doesn't
show up for class, Meyer might order all the running backs, the running
backs coach and his whole family to show up for a compensatory study
hall on a Friday night.

"If you feel responsible for letting down your whole position group,
your position coach and his family- that's pretty strong," Meyer said.
"I've had my six year old son come with me to a study hall and then tell
the guilty player, 'You want to explain to this six year old boy why he's
sitting here on a Friday night.' Having to explain to a six year old why
you missed class can be a much more powerful punishment that running stadium steps."

Practices are all about daily competitions. If the defense wins a certain
drill by point total (goal line scrimmages for instance), they retire early
to the locker room and a hot meal. The offense remains on the field and
stands behind a horizontal line. At the coaches' command, players have
to do sprints.

Every day, every practice, every drill has a winner and a loser. Winners
get rewarded. Losers get punished. Meyer knows that it's human
nature to avoid the shame of losing.

The way a player lines up turns into a competition. For example, running backs are each graded by coaches on how well they execute a 3-
point stance. The one with the best stance can move on while the player with the ugly stance has to sweat through more drills.
Even fun stuff like locker room tugs of war have winners and losers.
According to linebacker Brandon Siler, "You don't really concentrate

on how hard you are working because you just want to beat the dude in front of you."

The drill called "Circle of Life" stages one player against another in a ring formed by teammates. The players square off in a battle of toughness, with each trying to knock the other to the ground. One player grabs the other player somewhere near the joint of the elbow, then he pushes as his teammates circle around them and yell like hell rooting them on. The winner is celebrated, the loser humbled.

They have "Mat Drills" with groups of eight where they do wrestling type maneuvers where one player lays down and the other gets on top of him and holds him down. The object is for the one underneath to get up and off the mat. They have a champion of each group.

"The Pit" is much more demanding. It's an area of the practice field where strength coaches supervise drills designed to encourage players to practice through nagging aches and pains. Players there sometimes carry rocks and sandbags, run stadium steps and endure seemingly endless repetitions of sit-ups and push-ups.

Meyer also implemented "Hell Lifts," weightlifting sessions that usually begin late Friday night and last into the wee hours.

"Rookie stripes" are black stripes that are put on the helmet of each year's newcomer, who gets it removed when he "becomes a Gator."

"Joining the team doesn't make you a Gator," Meyer says. "It's much harder than that. You have to earn it."

The mind games haven't been confined to the practice field, either. During summer workouts last year, Meyer kicked players out of the locker room and told them they couldn't wear orange and blue or anything with the Gators logo on it.

"That was a big deal to us," former player Tate Casey said. "It was his way of sending us a message that we were taking everything for granted. This is the University of Florida. It's a privilege to be here and a privilege to play football here. Some guys might have lost sight of that, but he has that instilled into everyone now."

Meyer forces his assistants to know everything about the players they are coaching. The coaches literally possess a written accounting record that has every bit of personal information about the players they can muster.

"I had better not walk into a coach's meeting with Urban and not know a kid's mom's name, his girlfriend's name, the kid's cell-phone number, his likes, dislikes- everything," former assistant Doc Holliday said. When you know every nugget about a kid, you can see the problems coming long before they arrive.

"He is as demanding on the coaches as he is on the players," Holliday said. "You're going to be held accountable for everything you do. He wants a guy that instills discipline in the players."

The Florida program has a team leadership committee that consists of 5 seniors, 4 juniors, 3 sophomores, 2 freshmen, and one walk-on. The goal of the group is for the players to take ownership of the team. Players need to feel they have some stake in the team and some control over what happens.

"You have a tendency to complain less when it's your decision. When there is a problem, they will come to me with it," Meyer said.

An example of the leadership committee in action happened while Meyer was coaching at Utah and running back Marty Johnson got hit with a second DUI.

The committee came up with 12 criteria that Johnson had to do including being suspended for one full season, seeking alcohol counseling, graduating from college and not participating in scrimmages. He eventually did everything required of him to get reinstated and played a big role in Utah's undefeated 2004 season.

Talk a little bit about the Champion's Club program that you have had at each of your coaching stops.

John Wooden once said that you treat your players the way they deserve to be treated. You don't treat them all the same way. Our champion's club is for athletes who go to class, live their life the right way and contribute to the success of Florida football. If you do those three things, you get some nice gear as a reward- t-shirts, shorts, and hats, the whole deal.

We have a champion's banquet at the end of each quarter of the year. When I started the club at Bowling Green, I had a small budget so I met with the dining staff and told them I wanted "a nice prime rib dinner with fine linen and china and very nice tables in the nicest room on campus. We'll be doing that for 15 to 20 people. For the other 80, I want to order a really poor meal." For example, I wanted them to have some really bad hot dogs and half cooked hamburgers with stale buns served on paper plates.

During the banquets, members of the champions club get hugs and high fives and congratulations for making the club. You go sit down and take a seat with your laminated nameplate over there. Players that don't make it go sit over on the bleachers and eat their meal and watch the other guys. For the champions, if their prime rib isn't cooked right, they can send it back. If their tea is too sweet, they can send it back. We make sure their meal is fantastic.

The other guys get to think about their poor decisions. Those not in the club end up cleaning up for those who are. The guys who don't make the club get the idea of what they need to do to succeed, and we usually get more champions every quarter.

Ultimately, it's all about investment in the team. I've been part of football teams that have won in the fourth quarter and those that have lost in the forth quarter. There is a common denominator- the team that is most invested usually wins those game in the forth quarter. What I want for our team and our program is to shave the gap between the most invested and the least invested player and bring the average up to the top.

How do you develop toughness on the team?

Maybe you have to watch some film of some other guy who exhibits what toughness is. Our offensive line wasn't tough last year. So you can't watch film and say, "This is what I expect out of you every play." We don't have any film. So we're going to have to show other people's film. Donnie Young (an ex-Gator lineman on the 1996 national title team) is going to come in and talk to our offensive line. Donnie Young played with a level of toughness that was unequaled in his era from what I've heard.

Everybody ultimately wants a good program. We are far from that. The next thing they want is a good team, a group of unselfish people who will lay it on the line for each other. I'd rather have that than good players. I'd rather have a great team- unselfish players who love one another, care for each other and make the right decisions because they don't want to let each other down. The worst of these is merely to have good players.

Do you plan to go back to more fundamentals during spring and fall practices?

Everybody wants to talk scheme. They want to talk about the spread or the shotgun or the four-wide. What about blocking? Whether it's spread or not, eventually I've got to block you. The lost art in football in my mind is technique, it's the time spent on fundamentals, which is blocking and tackling.

We're building that into our conditioning. An offensive lineman running two gassers does nothing because you never run two gassers in a game. An offensive lineman gets in a football position and comes running off the ball for 10-yard bursts. We will do nothing other than football-related activities this year. After spring until August, we can't do anything with them. That's where the weight coaches have to be aware what we're teaching them so fundamentals increase during the summer.

What did you take away from your meeting with New England Patriots coach Bill Belichick?

That team doesn't have many superstars. They are the ultimate example of teamwork. How many off the field issues do they deal with in New England? You don't hear about their guys getting into trouble or arrested. They are a bunch of guys who stick together and like to hurt their opponents. That's what I want at the University of Florida.

The job description for our guys should include going to class, getting a degree, living right off the field and treating people with respect. If your job description as a player here doesn't fit into competing for and winning SEC championships every year, you are in the wrong place and need to get out.

How do you help develop the leadership qualities of a quiet personality type guy like quarterback Chris Leak?

When we first got here last year, Chris was a very average leader, but he has developed into an excellent one. Does that mean he has to stand up at the podium during meetings and yell and scream at the other players? No, but it does mean that he may have to walk across the hallway into someone's dorm room, close the door and find out what the heck is going on and why certain players are having issues. That's something he's not done in the past and is getting better at doing. When I first got here he was living right, but wasn't being that good of a leader. He needed to know what his teammates were doing after hours.

What are the most critical elements that go into the success of your program?

We have something we call "reward achievement," and I want our whole program based on effort. There is no such thing as luck. If there was, the assistant coaches could walk around with a rabbit's foot in their pocket and not really have to work. We believe in hard work.

There is a sign in our weight room that is a paraphrase of the Michael Jordan quote, "It's why we train with the passion we do- so that the games are easy."

Interview excerpted from Urban Meyer booster club speech, Orlando Sentinel and Gainesville Sun newspapers.

- 8 -

MICHELLE AKERS: WORLD CUP WINNING SUCCESS STRATEGIES

Michelle Akers was one of the star players on the USA Women's Soccer teams that won two World Cup Championships and an Olympic Gold Medal. She was named the Women's Player of the Century by FIFA.

Talk about the importance of team chemistry.

That is something that we really work on. Team chemistry is an important and deciding factor in determining your place on the team. If you don't fit in on the team or cause problems, you are going to get booted. That is well known amongst our team and is a high priority with the players and coaching staff.

Every player on the USA women's national team has to contribute to more than just on the soccer field. We realize that winning takes more than just performance. It really makes a difference in whether you are serving your teammates, fun to be around, generous, polite, and not causing problems. That is one of the factors that made us such a good team. We talk about it up front first. That makes the leadership on the team very strong. The veterans model good behavior in practices, on the road in all kinds of conditions and the youngsters just kind of follow suit.

We have our team dinners. At our training residency in Orlando, everyone lives in different places so once or twice a month we will get together at someone's house and have a team dinner and just hang out. Other times teammates play golf or go to Disney World. Some days we will have team building exercises at a ropes course. All of these activities cultivate team chemistry.

Do players have to be friends off field to have good team chemistry?

Not necessarily. You don't need to be buddies with everyone. There are some people you just don't like or don't get along with. Try to be professional and just play. The friendship part is not going to grow any further. But there is a line drawn when a player disturbs team chemistry because of their behavior or inability to get along with teammates. At that point, that player may be asked to leave the team. Most everyone on the team were friends, and we genuinely liked each other. We run for each other, play for each other and it is just an incredibly unique team in that aspect.

What role does the coach play in the motivational process?

I am intrinsically motivated. I really don't rely on my coach to get me fired up. So that is probably not as important for me as it may be for other players. I recognize different leadership styles. What I have learned is that each coach definitely leads the team in different ways. It is important is to treat players as individuals and not as a group.

Are there different motivation approaches between male and female athletes?

One of my past coaches had this theory of how to teach and motivate female players. He has been extremely successful, but I disagree on the blanket theory of how to coach women. There are some generalities in men vs. women. For instance, guys respond more favorably when they get yelled at than do girls. And you are not going to motivate a girl to play better by telling them that they stink, and you should just quit soccer because you don't cut it. A guy might get ticked off and play harder. There is only a small minority of girls that would get fired up with that strategy.

I think it is good to be well versed in the generalities of training and coaching. Male vs. female differences ultimately comes down to understanding how a player takes criticism and how they are wired so the coach can press those buttons to maximize their performance.

How do you learn what a player's hot buttons are?

It's the process of getting to know someone. You can't ask them two questions and understand what rocks their world. It takes time, and those players have to get to know the coach as well in order to respond. A relationship has to be built.

I think the coach can set the standard and initiate the process throughout the getting-to-know-you period. Even after that, it is important for the coach to be consistent and also communicate and lay out his or her expectations and goals. The coach should take time to get to know the player and find out what gets them going.

I understand you work with a sport psychologist. What psychological techniques does she utilize when assisting the team and coaching staff?

Some examples are imagery, visualization, and audio and video CD/DVDs with the player's choice of music. She has one-on-one time with players. She deals with the coaching staff and gives them tips on where we are and what needs to be done, and how they can help us perform. She does team building sessions.

The topics that she has chosen to discuss with the team the last several years have mostly been about confidence, believing in yourself, and celebrating your own talent, but realizing that you can't do it alone and that everybody has their own gift. Everybody brings something to the table, and you are not going to win anything on your own.

She talks about setting boundaries and saving me-time, looking at soccer as a component of your life. For example, if you look at a pie and your soccer wedge is 90% of who you are, then you have some problems. You are probably not very happy. She reminds and teaches people that there is more to you than the game. For a time, the soccer portion will be larger than some other portions, but overall you are striving to give equal attention to all these different areas, and it is up to you to set the boundaries on what is going on in your life to keep those areas filled up.

As a professional athlete you have to deal with being pushed and pulled in many different directions. So you really have to fight to maintain those boundaries. A lot of players have a problem with that because they are trying to please the media or please their sponsor, and they end up just getting stomped. So a lot of times, that is a hard lesson to learn.

You have had to overcome a lot of injuries in your career. Discuss how you cope with them and your mental approach to recovery.

First, take a look at who I am and then you will understand how I respond to injuries. I am an all or nothing person. Physically, I'm not afraid of much. When I get injured, it is like a little bump. What motivates me are obstacles and adversity. So the bigger the challenge in front of me, the more motivated I am in all aspects of my life.

The harder the situation is, the worse the injury is, and the more difficult the competition is all serve as a fire and a challenge. That gets me going. My attitude is, "Let's see what I can do with this. Throw anything at me and I'll go after it."

I have had 12 or 13 knee surgeries and head injuries. My last one was a facial fracture - a pretty serious injury that required surgery. Those kinds of things serve as motivators for me.

I still have to step on the field and deal with the possibility of getting injured. Sometimes, I come back quicker from an injury than I should. I take risks. Sometimes that is not smart, but it is also an advantage in a way because I get right back into the swing of things. I've changed somewhat now. In the past, I came back so quickly from injuries because soccer was the big portion in my life, and without it I was a little bit lost.

Talk about how you battled Chronic Fatigue Syndrome (a disease which drains the person of energy and causes other physical problems).

At my worst point, I was barely able to function. It was an extreme effort to do laundry, prepare a meal, or ride an exercise bike for five minutes. There was neck and back pain, dizziness, water retention, night sweats, poor sleep, and many other symptoms. The road to recovery was a slow progression.

Here are the steps that I attribute to my return to health: 1) Change in diet. I cut down on caffeine and drank more water. I ate small balanced meals 4-5 times a day to maintain my energy. 2) Smarter, shorter, supervised work-outs. I adjusted my exercise routine to how my body was feeling and pushed less. I sometimes would over-train on my own. I had a conditioning coach monitor my physical symptoms daily who forced me to be accountable. We devised an exercise program to get me back on my feet and pulled back when I wasn't responding well. 3) Physical and massage therapy. Massage helps blood circulation and muscle fatigue and promotes healing. Physical therapy helps relieve muscle spasms and alleviates pain. 4) Stress Reduction. We choose how to respond to the emotions we feel. When an "energy-sapping" emotion flared up (anger, anxiousness, guilt or fear) I took hold of it and refused to let it control my energy reserve. Choose to confront and overcome these types of emotion even though it's not easy. By recognizing negative feelings early, you can head off a lot of physical repercussions that slow your recovery and sense of wellbeing.   5) Spirituality I rekindled my relationship with Christ. This was a major step toward my recovery. My faith is the center of my ongoing recovery and how I deal with Chronic Fatigue Syndrome on a daily basis. Everyone who is chronically ill has been forced to look at a "higher power." I learned I did not have the strength to carry on under my own power. I wondered what all this was for. The disease brought me to my knees. I asked if there was a purpose for this humiliation and suffering? God answered all those questions and provided me with the strength, courage, and peace to live and overcome in sickness or health.

What role does your faith play in your athletic performance?

Being a Christian allows me to have a trust there- have a confidence that I am protected. Nothing is going to happen to me that I can't handle as long as I have done the homework. When I'm playing a game I know that God's hand is going to be on me, and it has been. I have experienced it enough to know that if I go out there and get injured again, I'm going to be OK.

- 9 -

MIKE CANDREA: DEVELOPING THE MENTAL TOUGHNESS OF CHAMPIONS

Arizona Softball Coach Mike Candrea has led the Wildcats to 9 NCAA championships and has taken the team to 21 straight College World Series.

Talk about the mental game as it relates to your sport.

Softball is a game of relaxation. The more relaxed you are, the better you can perform. Softball is a little different in the sense that there is a lot of downtime, so athletes have to learn to be able to handle that downtime where you can focus, concentrate, and then relax. Focus, concentration and relaxation are the series of steps that athletes go through during each game. Athletes have to concentrate and focus on every pitch, and that becomes very difficult unless you know how to not let your mind wander.

Do you have any specific exercises to improve concentration that you teach your athletes?

We try to do various things on how to relax. Sometimes you tell kids to relax, but you don't give them the ways to accomplish the request. The first thing is controlling your breathing. Your breathing will tell you when you start racing as an athlete. Usually your breaths get really shallow. I think a lot of relaxation in our game comes from confidence. I think the more confident you are as an athlete, the more relaxed you can play.

Probably the most important thing in our game is self-talk. What are athletes telling themselves when they are on the on deck circle? What are they telling themselves when the ball is hit to them? Self-talk becomes a really big thing at our level because softball is still pretty much a pitching dominated game. Hitting is very difficult in baseball and even more difficult in softball. So I think that anything that you can do as a coach to keep your kids build confidence helps.

Routines are important. Our batting practice or our pre-game routine is the same, and it is something that we take from our practices. No matter where we are in the country or what field we are on, we have something that is very familiar to us and our pre-game never changes. Routines, breathing exercises and just being aware of what your body is doing will help you learn to relax.

You've coached 9 championship teams. Are there common elements or certain traits that all of your teams had?

Obviously there is a level of ability you have to have. But with that level of ability there is a common trait of team chemistry. I don't think that anyone can underestimate the importance of team chemistry, and I'm not talking about something that is fake, something that you are trying to produce but something that is real. Everyone understands that we work very, very hard. I pride myself and we try to pride our team on our work ethic. I think the ability to handle adversity, the ability to worry more about the process than the end result is a part of it. One thing we never do is talk about national championships. We never talk about being in the top 10. What we talk about is, "What can we do today to become a better team?" We try to keep it at that level and then good things will happen for you. If you overlook that process you are very vulnerable for setting yourself up for failure.

Lacking the fear of failure is another component. One of the things we pride our team on is being aggressive. And sometimes you are going to make a mistake and if it is an aggressive mistake then you don't worry about it. If it is a passive mistake, then that is something that we worry about.

In teaching, when you are trying to correct mistakes, do you have a certain way that you communicate with your players?

Obviously if somebody has made a mistake, they are aware of it so they don't have to be reminded. I think the key is to use it as a teaching moment. If a kid makes a mistake, it is important that sometime very soon after that, you sit down and talk about what they have done and you give them a way of correcting it. A lot of times coaches will tell kids that they have screwed up, but they will never tell them how to correct it. You have got to be careful because the one thing we are trying to teach is confidence. Depending on how you handle that athlete will definitely have an effect on how confident they feel, and what their self-esteem is like. The higher the self-esteem of an athlete, the more chance of them overachieving. If you, as a coach, lower a team's self-esteem then I think that you will find a team that is going to underachieve.

Earlier you said relaxation was very important in softball. Do you ever see any benefit in giving your team a pep talk, or is that something that you try to avoid?

I think timing is probably the most important thing. When it comes to pep talks, I think sometimes at certain times throughout the year, an inspirational talk can be effective.

Can you give me an example of when is the best time?

Usually it is a time where I feel that we are underachieving- when we are possibly going through the motions, and we have kind of lost track of the process of what it truly takes for us to reach our goals. I think kids need reminders.

A lot of the times it may be after a win and very seldom after a loss. If I am going to be truly critical of my team, a lot of times it will be after a win. Because I think sometimes people look at a win and think they did everything right. Well that's not the case if you are a perfectionist. The process, how we win, and how we lose makes the difference in my eyes. We can lose and play very well. If we get beat then that is something different than if we beat ourselves- that warrants an opportunity to look back and see where we want to go from here and what we need to do to get there.

If you are the type that talks too much, what you say becomes less effective to your athletes. Timing is so important. It's hard to stay by the book when you do you give a pep talk. In the past when I feel like our team chemistry may not be good or we're not quite playing as a unit, I would bring every kid in and individually talk to them and kind of find out where they are coming from.

It gives me an opportunity to recap, and sometimes it may be to give them some criticism and some things on which they need to improve. Sometimes it gives me an opportunity to say, "Hey, you are doing a good job." Sometimes as coaches we don't give out the praise as much as we do the criticism. And I think that there has got to be a balance there, because you are dealing with the most precious commodity in our game, which is confidence.

For instance, take batting practice. My job as a coach is to make sure that our hitters are confident when the game begins. In practice, it is my job to challenge our hitters. Prior to a game, that pre-game is a set routine and that doesn't change and builds confidence.

Do you let your own individual athletes develop their own routines, or do you help them structure it?

There is a lot of structure in it, but within the structure there are opportunities to deal with the individual. For instance, when we are hitting sometimes I will tell a kid to take as many cuts as she needs to feel good. For some kids, it may be 5 or 10 cuts- for others, many more.

I'm not real big on getting everyone up at 8:00 in the morning and having them eat a team meal. Because I think that everyone prepares differently for games. If I'm not a breakfast eater and you are going to force me to eat on the road, then I'm probably not going to feel as good.

You want to keep the routines of those kids to as close to what they do everyday when you are traveling. Sometimes we will pull a team meal to maybe break things up and have some fun. I remember one year at the College World Series I thought our team was a little tight. I think they were starting to feel the pressure, so I took our team out for a team meal and then we went out and played goofy golf and rode bumper cars for about 30 to 40 minutes.

Usually you play your best softball when you are having fun. When the game is not fun anymore, you can see it in the athlete. One of my biggest goals as a softball coach is to "live a little" because we don't have anybody walking out of our high school that is going to make 3 million a year. So I want to make sure that they enjoy that process as much as possible. They can play softball and get their education paid for in full.

The toughest thing about repeating as champions is to keep the enthusiasm. Once you reach your goals, you have the tendency to not be quite as hungry.

Part of my job as a coach and one of my main goals is to bring in athletes that have the same aspirations as I do. My other job is to get rid of any athletes that don't have them. Sometimes you have to make decisions that aren't really popular, but in the long run you are going to win consistently, because you have better people who are on the same page.

What do you tell your players in the pre-season when you have that #1 ranking to deal with?

We don't really talk about it. Right now our program is kind of expected to compete for the national championship every year, and we know that there is a process that you have to go through to make that happen. We don't talk about the past and don't get tied up in the things of which we have no control. When you start worrying about rankings and stats, sometimes you end up playing the wrong game. That's one area that I'm different from other coaches. Softball and baseball are so statistics-oriented. I don't post stats, and our kids don't know what they are hitting. The only thing that really counts is, "are we getting better each day?"

When you are out recruiting a young lady, do you look for a certain type of personality or attitude in the very beginning?

I like winners. I like kids that have the ability to come through in a clutch, so I always look at game situations where the game is on the line. I want to know, "How does this kid react during clutch situations? Is she the kind of kid that is consistently driving in the winning run?" If so, you have a kid that obviously can handle the pressure of the game and has the confidence that it takes to play at this level.

Obviously you face a different level of competition from high school to college.

The other thing in our level is that I want kids that aren't in awe of this level of competition. I'm looking for kids that have played against tough competition in high school. When you get a kid that has not played at that level, you have to give them time to grow. I like kids that are confident, and have some sense of discipline and direction.

Do you get this information from your personal contact with the kids or from their coaches in high school?

My personal contact with the athletes is vital. One of the most important times for me in the recruiting process is the home visit. When you go into a home, you can pretty much tell what the kid is going to be like. You can kind of see where they come from. If they haven't had any direction at home, do you think you can change that in a year? No! But if you can see in the home that there is definitely some structure and people put a price on being successful, then I think that you have a kid that will be able to achieve at the highest levels.

- 10 -

JIMMY JOHNSON: CREATING A WINNING ATMOSPHERE

Former Miami Hurricanes and Dallas Cowboys Head Football Coach Jimmy Johnson is one of the only coaches to lead his teams to both a College National Championship and 2 Super Bowl titles.

What are your primary responsibilities as a leader and head coach?

It is my number one duty to make sure I bring out the best in everyone around me. It's not just me telling others what they need to do. It's creating an atmosphere where they can grow, expand and also give input into how we are going to accomplish our goals.

If I have everyone in our organization operating at a maximum level, then I've accomplished my number one goal.

How do you create that winning atmosphere?

Let's say I wake up on the wrong side of the bed and my back aches and I'm not in a very good mood. If I bring that poor attitude to the field with me at practice, it is certainly going to carry over to them. We will probably end up having a wasted day of practice. I've got to be in control of my mind and emotions so that I feel better than anyone else around me. I need to set the example of both enjoying my job and working hard because that attitude filters through to everyone else.

What advice would you have to a coach who has just gone through a really bad season and is feeling like a failure?

Their premise is wrong. If they feel like a failure, then they already took the first step toward being a failure. I like the phrase, "Treat a person as he is, and he will become what he is. Treat him the way you

71

want him to become and he will." That doesn't just apply to others, it applies to yourself. It's very important that you treat yourself as a winner. I used to tell the players, "Guys, we need to exhibit a little false enthusiasm. Because pretty soon, that will turn into real enthusiasm."

It's so important to be able to control your own mind. I've often said that the strongest people in the world are not the 500-pound bench pressers, but the ones who have control over their own mind. They get up in the morning with a smile on their face and tell themselves, "Today is a great day, and I am going to accomplish great things. I'm going to have a great attitude and work harder than the next guy. Good things are going to happen for me today." That really is the first step to achieving success.

What are some practical ways you can develop a positive mental outlook?

I think it's important to have some point in the day when you can reflect. For me, I like to jog and then walk for a while. I don't work out so hard where I think about how much pain I am in. This is my time to think and ask myself questions like, "What do I need to do today? How can I get better? How can I make my team get better? How can I influence the people who work around me and the players in a positive way?" Taking the time to gather your thoughts is a key to long term success.

Where did your success philosophy come from?

It started back in my college days as a psychology major. Over the years I listened to other coaches and motivational speakers like Zig Ziglar and borrowed one or two key concepts from each of these people. Over time, I was able to blend other people's thoughts into my own philosophy. No matter who I was dealing with- my secretary, trainer, strength coach, or the players - I would try to treat them as winners and communicate with them in a manner that brought out their best.

Where did your excellent people skills come from?

It started from a selfish perspective. I always would think, "How would I want someone to talk with me and deal with me?" I wanted people to treat me as a winner.

The psychology of this becomes a self-fulfilling prophecy. Over time, you treat them the way you want to be treated, and they become what you want them to become.

How did you help change player attitudes during that 1-15 season with the Cowboys?

I remember we were 1-7 and had a chance to beat Phoenix, but came up just short. I knew that we needed to start taking little strides that first year to lay the groundwork for later success. After the game, one of our players was laughing and joking with a guy from the opposing team. I just about lost it. I told the guy to get his rear end into the locker room. He asked me why I was so upset and told me, "We've already lost 7, what's one more?"

I told the whole team after the game, "If you don't have a sick feeling after losing a game like this, when you come up short, then you are losing something of yourself. You are losing your own pride. Don't be involved with the sport at this level if you can accept losing. I don't care what our record is and what happens from here on. We are looking further down the road and we have to have a winning attitude." The players saw how hard my assistants and I took the losses. That planted the seed of an attitude change that sunk in over time.

Another example of developing a winning attitude happened after we achieved some success. That year, we had locked up home field advantage in the play-offs. We had a "meaningless" game to end the season, and we lost it. On the plane ride back to Dallas, players were cutting up and joking like we had won the game. I went back and told them, "Hey guys, you have to understand that every time you walk on the field, you are forming habits. You conduct yourselves in a certain way. If you put a half way effort into something, because you think it is 'meaningless,' you are setting yourself up for failure later. We are always either getting better or worse. You all took a step in the wrong direction because the attitude was, 'this isn't an important game.' We got worse out there today. Every game is an opportunity to be the best you can be."

How did you communicate with your players at halftime?

As a head coach, you have to be careful in that you must convey thoughts and information in a brief time period. After a two or three minute cooldown period, the assistants will go through the technical aspects of correcting mistakes for about six or seven minutes. I would take the last two or three minutes to give them a final thought to plant the seed in their mind of what was going to happen in the second half. I would predict what was going to happen.

For example, we were playing Buffalo in the Super Bowl. In the two weeks leading up to the game, we had stressed how much of fight the Bills were going to give us and that we should plan to be in a close game, but that we would win in the end. I told our offense that we've played poorly and made a lot of mistakes, but are still in position to win. Now it's time to execute like we have all season. I told the defense, "Now we take charge. Now we will take the initiative and make things happen. We're going to cause a turnover that will put us right back in the position we want to be. When we scored to make it even, the seeds had been planted in our team's mind that, 'hey this game is now going to turn our way.'"

I usually didn't rant and rave at halftime- although there is a time and place for those types of speeches. I would give the fire and brimstone speech when we were playing a team that we were clearly superior to talent wise, but we just went through the motions in the first half. Most of my halftime talks were analytical, and my attempt to plant the seeds of success by saying what would happen in the second half.

What would you have done if in the Bills game, your team had not gotten the turnover that you predicted would happen?

With our aggressive style of defense and Buffalo's high risk offense, a turnover was a pretty safe bet. The key in sports is to seize the momentum shifts. There are so many big plays in the course of a game. It's the team that is best able to handle those psychological swings that would most often win. We tried to downplay the negative swings and really build on the positive plays. I liked it when our guys would show emotion and throw their arms in the air and hug one another. When our opponents saw that exuberance, they would feel like, 'hey, we're getting beat here. They are the better team.' That exuberance worked for us and also against our opponents by helping shift the psychological momentum more in our favor.

Interview excerpted from the Peter Lowe success series audio tape.

- 11 -

BETH ANDERS: BEST PLAYER/COACH COMMUNICATION METHODS

Old Dominion University Field Hockey coach Beth Anders has led her teams to 9 national championships and has compiled over 500 victories.

Communication with players is so very important. Describe some of the ways you try to get through to them.

In communicating with players, the main thing is to listen. I watch them and I listen, not just verbally, but also by watching their body language. Consistency in your messages is important. I don't say one thing and then do another. I don't change that much. I try to tell them exactly what I mean. They always have an opportunity to respond and say what they think.

You just try to treat each player as a person. You definitely have to gain that trust or that bond where both sides would do anything for each other.

For all the championship teams, we had a certain trust. If I told them to put their left foot forward, they would think that was probably the best way to execute. They wouldn't ask the purpose or try to understand the purpose or think they had another way that was better. It's not that I don't want to be challenged. From time to time, I ask them to do just that. But I do think that there has to be a tremendous bond of trust between the player and the coach.

When you have a conflict between two players, what are the strategies you use to resolve them?

First of all, you watch it. Then you see if they can resolve it, depending on how major it is. You let it go to a certain degree because these kids love the competition. It's important not to take sides. Let the players know what you want for the outcome.

For example, you could explain why you want the defender to defend a certain way. You address the girls so that they both go in the right direction together.

Or you can ask them what the problem is and then you don't really give them the answer, but you get them to give you the answer. Giving kids the answer is not the solution. I think you empower kids by giving them the ability to think, giving them the ability to understand the game, and giving them the tools of the game.

I don't try to make one person right and the other person wrong. It is a win-win type of thing.

Example: I'll ask them '"Where is the ball?" After they both give the correct answer, then I would ask, '"Now where is your opponent?" Then I would say, "OK, what is the best way to cover that space?" Usually they'll both come to the same conclusion.

Honestly, sometimes conflict is not bad. It is not always bad if you use it in a positive way and can get a positive result. The bottom line is you have to get to the solution that is going to get them to operate effectively.

Talk about correcting mistakes during a competition.

One of my girls was a defender on the goal line at the beginning of the game and during a penalty corner, she went to the wrong side of the cage. The girl scored on the side of the cage she should have been on. I didn't say anything. It's not that I didn't want to make the correction, but I didn't want her to be thinking too much about the mistake. When she came back to her position, she just looked at me and said, "I won't do it again."

I said, "You're OK. Keep going." With three seconds left in the game she saved a shot while staying in the right place. It was awesome because this girl wasn't one of our best athletes. She was just a great kid who kept on fighting. There was never a point when she was going to quit.

In listing your most important ingredients for success, what would be at the top of your list?

It would be hard to say that one characteristic is more important for success than another. I know you can't have trust without communication, and trust goes with respect. You must have athletes willing to prepare, to accept responsibility and to learn.

I don't play games. I don't believe in that. My philosophy is to teach the fundamentals of the game. I do have a system that gives kids roles on the field.

You mentioned having trouble getting through to one group of kids. What did you alter in your coaching style to reach them?

I couldn't challenge this group as hard as I had in the past. So I had to figure out a way to get them to the next level without going about it the way that had been successful for 12 years. I'm not sure if that is attributed to the change in athletes at that point or just that certain group.

I couldn't push them as hard, but you can't be good if you aren't challenged. Athletes have to get out of their "comfort zone." You have to be able to risk it. This group was not comfortable with that, and it drove me nuts. So I didn't apply as much pressure as I normally would with other teams. They couldn't handle nearly any verbal pressure, so I had to become much more patient, and eventually things worked out.

What is your philosophy regarding pep talk speeches? Are they just to be used once in a while or not at all?

I always talk to the players before every game, either the night before or the day before. It doesn't have to be long, but you have to know your individuals and say exactly what gets them to believe in themselves and feel like "Yes, we can do this!"

Pep talks only maybe work for the first 10 minutes of a game. I think you have to tell players the truth. Once they believe in themselves, it brings them into focus about what they are going to do in a game. It gets them to think about what they are going to do.

In the night before the game, do you talk to them specifically about what their challenges are for the next game?

It's not always the same. You have to listen and watch the players for the whole week. Are they confident? A day of game pep talk is not going to fix something that is broken. Talking is not necessarily going to get you anywhere except to bring focus into what the players should do. It could be the tactics or technique of the game or it could be the mental part. You try to give them what they need. Everything that comes from me comes from the heart. It comes from what I see. Rarely have I said the same thing twice.

Talk a little about the athlete's personal development.

Yes, there is a big difference between winners and champions. And I want everybody to leave here knowing that they are a winner. You can only do that by developing the total person.

I want them to be a better person from the day they come here to the day they leave. And when you are a better person, you can make your own decisions, believe in yourself, and stand on your own two feet. You know how to relate and communicate with others.

Once you develop these qualities in people, the rest is easy or at least more than doable. I have a background in teaching. It would be very hard for me to do what I do now without that background. I taught seven years in high school and want to develop the total person, not just the field hockey player. Another selling point is that I'm mature, consistent and try to be very fair. I'm always available. There is not one minute of the day when if one of my athletes needs me, she can't reach me. If I can't help her, then I will direct her to someone else who can.

Were there key ingredients all of your championship teams had that make them so good?

They all had different personalities. One of the main things they did was they challenged me to coach them. When you get a challenge from your players to coach them, it puts everybody on the same page and you are now working together towards something.

Because they challenged me, I got them sharp on one thing, and then they challenged me again.

In "Mental Toughness Training" by Jim Loehr, he has four markers about mental toughness, and I think they had those. They were resilient- they could bounce back very quickly from mistakes. They had a tremendous inner-strength, especially as the pressure increased. I believe that comes through preparation. They definitely were responsive. They were able to remained focused under pressure, and they had flexibility. They were willing to prepare, and I think the other thing is that they loved the game. Not every day was a ball, but they had fun. They also had the ability to respect each other. I don't think that they were best friends, but they did respect each other.

- 12 -

HERB BROOKS: MIRACLE MOTIVATION

In his final interview, Olympic "Miracle" ice hockey coach Herb Brooks shared his coaching philosophies with the producers of the movie. Here are some highlights.

Creating team morale: The team-building thing was huge. We had to overcome loads of obstacles. We had to have enthusiasm, comradeship, and great morale in the locker room. I worked their tails off. The guys had to re-invent themselves. The training was more intense than they were used to. The style of play was entirely different than they had played before. They had to develop a hybrid style that incorporated aspects of European and Canadian hockey. So first the guys had to have good personal attitudes, plus they had to be in an environment where it was conducive to team building. We had a set of players who could all adapt to a new style of play. They were willing to be interchangeable parts that made a greater whole. They were a tough group of kids psychologically. I wanted to keep them all on the bubble as long as possible. I didn't want to give anyone the impression that they were safe on this hockey club (and could be sent off as they all knew that one of them would during training camp).

Motivating Goalie Jim Craig: I played mind games with Jim Craig right into the very end, one day before the official start of the games. I knew I had to tweak him again even though he was playing solid. So I said, "Jimmy, I screwed up." He asked me what I meant. I said, "I think I have played you too long. Your curve ball is hanging. It's not your fault. It's my fault. I see elements of your game where you are playing tight. I take responsibility for that." I told him I was going to play the back up for half the game to give him some work. I said, "I see some flaws in your game. I'm kicking myself for not noticing sooner. It's not your fault. I've played you too much." He came back at me hard, "That's my job. I'll show you what I can do, blah blah, blah." During the final exhibition against Russia, I yanked him. He came to me after the game, and he was livid. But I knew what I had with Craig and I had to give him one last little tweak to get his game to another level. I ended up playing him right through every game of the Olympics. After we won the Gold, he comes up and points a finger at my chest and says, "I showed you. Didn't I coach?" I said, "Yes you did Jimmy. You did a helluva job."

Challenging Rob McClanahan (and the entire team): We just lost to the Russians in the final exhibition 10-3, so I had to immediately pump the guys back up. I was talking to our team doctor and told him that I had to do something to shake these boys up. They were frozen out there. It just so happened that McClanahan hurt his leg. I had coached him for 4 years and knew exactly what button to press with this kid. So I took the tough road. He had been hurt, but the doctor said it wouldn't be any worse if he played. So I told him, "It's too bad about the injury, but a bruise on the leg is a long way from the heart kid. He said, "I can't even sit down." Then you should stand up, you candy-ass. McClanahan replies, "What did you call me?" Then I said, "You heard me." He gets up and yells, "Do you want me to play hurt?" I replied, "No, I want you to be a hockey player." Then the other guys have to hold him back as he starts screaming at me as I leave the room.

The whole locker room was really upset. It could have gone the other way. The team could have divided after this. It (the motivational ploy) was a gamble. So Rob goes ballistic and the whole locker room wakes up. I walked out and told the assistant coach, "Now I think they are ready to go." McClanahan couldn't sit down, so he stood up on the bench, but he played hurt and he played well. He had a lot of heart.

Pushing Jack O'Callahan: He was very important to the team chemistry. He was a smart, charismatic guy, and I used him to motivate the rest of the team. I told him, "Listen, when I talk to you as OC, the message goes out to everyone. But when I call you 'Jack,' you will know that I am unhappy with your play." He could take being abused a little bit. So when the rest of the team saw me call him Jack, they would say, "Oh crap, he is being hard on the OC today. We better watch it." When

I pushed OC, he would ratchet his game up and do a little more in practice. The team would follow his lead. That was a key part of the team-building thing.

On skating the team hard after the Norway exhibition game during training for the games: T here was a lot of locker room talk around that time that was distracting the team. They were talking about agents and turning pro, and they were pissing and moaning about some of the things we were doing training wise. I knew I had to draw a line in the sand early on in the process. In the Norway game, they clearly were not taking things seriously. They didn't respect the opposition. They weren't playing with the necessary intensity- with or without the puck on offense or defense. They basically took the night off.

Before the game, I told them we will get a good work-out now or after the game. I think they thought I was kidding. Would I do it again? (Skate the team after the game until some were vomiting). I don't know. The players later said that was one of the moments that they came together and realized it's us against the world (as opposed to the various college programs they represented). After that drill, they all realized that they had to come to practice ready to bust their asses. I wasn't going to give them a night off and let them think, "It's ok boys, we had one of those games." Every single day was important to building toward our long-range goal. I was always going to hold them to high standards. I think they took away the message, "we better not ever let up and always be ready to go full throttle."

Creating high standards: Lots of the guys on the team were college All-Americans who had not been pushed really hard in the past. I wasn't trying to put greatness into anyone; I was trying to pull it out. Some coaches try to put it in because they think they have all the answers. You have to believe in your team, set high standards and pull greatness out of them.

On adapting the US style of play: When I interviewed for the job, I told the US Olympic committee, we can't be the same old style. All they used to do was take all the great college athletes, raise some money and then go the Olympic games and get whacked. I told them we had to change the way we approached everything. When you have competition without preparation, there is no real involvement from the players. We had to develop these people. We did a lot of things in our training and preparation to get them out of their comfort zone - both psychologically and physiologically. We had the best-conditioned club, outside the Soviets in the world.

Learning from the Europeans: I asked myself the question, "Will we be successful playing a North American style game in the Olympics against the Europeans?" I made it a point to steal ideas from other clubs. What makes the Soviets and Czeks and Swedes so great? The answer was style of play and tremendous conditioning. What would happen for the US teams in the past is that they would play great for one or two periods, then hit a wall and die. They could no longer keep up. I was going to make sure we would not hit that wall.

Selecting the US squad: I had done a year and a half of research on players going into the Olympic festival (where players were trying out to make the team). I had a very good idea going in. There were a few guys I wasn't sure would make it. Team captain Mike Eruzione was one. I wanted to see how he would do in this environment. He was by far not our best hockey player, but he was a great guy and a good leader.

Team rules: There was a guy who showed up at training camp with a beard. So a few days later other guys started to grow beards. I told the team, "About these beards, here is the rules - whoever showed up at camp with a beard can keep one. The rest of you guys are wannabes, so no beards. I gave the guys some leeway. I never had curfews. My thinking I didn't want to have to suspend any of my best players for curfew violations.

On Winning the Gold: This was a team that accomplished something totally as a group, not as a set of individuals. The top sporting achievement of the last 100 years was given to the 1980 hockey team, not an individual. The most gratifying thing to me is having a group being recognized as opposed to say, Michael Jordan. They were all great athletes, but it was the synergy that transformed their talents into something much more.

The preceding interview was excerpted from the Miracle movie bonus documentary.

- 13 -

KIRK FERENTZ: KEEPING A PROGRAM AT A CONSISTENT HIGH LEVEL

University of Iowa football coach Kirk Ferentz has led the program to two Big Ten titles and 9 straight bowl appearances.

You've had a great run at Iowa. What are some of the factors that have led to your consistent levels of success? Did the teams share common traits to make them successful?

First and foremost, we've had a great group of players to work with at Iowa. They are proud and competitive guys who have been willing to work hard. Our best players have been our best guys, which have given us great examples to point to for our younger athletes. Second, we have a tremendous staff here- they are excellent teachers who have done a great job of developing our players, not only as football players, but also as people. We've had great continuity on the staff. The guys persevered through the tough times and stayed motivated toward improving.

At first it was a struggle at Iowa. How did you keep the team positive at that point?

Even though we had a 1-10 record our first season, we had upperclassmen who stayed positive and worked as hard as they could. The highlight of that season was the week after we lost badly to Wisconsin (who won the Big 10 conference that year). In our 11th week we had our best week of practice and lost a very close game to a strong Minnesota team. That was an important period for us. We had a bunch of players with good attitudes who kept working through the tough times.

What are your thoughts on motivating the entire team throughout the course of a season? How do you strike a balance between pushing too hard and knowing when to back off?

There are a lot of variables involved here. It depends on how the season is going and on the make-up of the team, both physically and mentally. It's never constant. As coaches, we all have to realize the ups and downs a team experiences during the season and be sensitive to where the team's state of mind is at any given point during the year.

Motivating the team starts during the recruiting stage. We want players who have the right priorities and right goals. We want guys who know that for good things to become a reality, it requires that they pay a pretty high price. It boils down to guys working to get a degree, living right and playing hard, and if they are willing to work, motivation takes care of itself.

Do you do any off-season team building exercises to bring a team closer together and perform as a unit? What do you see as the keys to building team unity?

In the summertime, we encourage our players to take a leadership role and organize simple team outings like a softball game, bowling tournament or picnic. We like our players to organize it and execute it on their own.

One of the only structured activities we do takes place right after spring ball. We have a softball extravaganza where the different classes play one another, and the coaches play the seniors.

During pre-season practice, we bring in various speakers to address different issues.

We also have a leadership group, which seems to be fairly common now. Each class has representatives. I meet with them, we chat about topics that are important to them and I discuss some things that I feel are important as well.

Could you share a few examples here of what was discussed in these meetings?

We will visit about anything important to our players that they want to propose to me. Also, it gives me an opportunity to bounce ideas off them and get feedback from a group of very respected players. A few items we discuss would be procedure for pre-season practices, approach to our bye week, thoughts on bowl game schedules, trip logistics and also discipline topics- both serious and not so serious matters. Typically, when it comes to discipline ideas, the players tend to be harder on each other than you might expect.

How do you handle adversity during games? For example, let's say the other team scores two touchdowns early in a game and puts you at a deficit. What would be some of the things you might say to keep them mentally focused and positive?

We try to take the approach that we are always striving for consistency. But we realize that in sports, like life, things can take a turn for the better or worse. Sometimes, things go too easily early, which can be as tough as facing a poor start. No matter what the situation, the key is to focus on the task at hand. We talk to our players about not worrying about what the score is or what the weather conditions are- we just want to go out and perform. There might be a five-minute segment of the game that doesn't go exactly as we planned. But we encourage them to stay on the course and stay on the path that got us where we are. And if the whole game goes poorly and we lose, we talk about rebounding the next week.

We cite examples of other teams that have faced similar situations. For example, if it is half-time and we are down 20 points or up 15, we look back on what some other teams have done and say, "hey, so and so was down and they came back to win." or "this other team was up two touchdowns and got complacent and lost the game."

We don't talk so much about winning as much as giving our best performance. That way, the scoreboard or individual adverse instances during games lose some of their importance.

What is your view on team rules and what part, if any, do the athletes have in making them and enforcing them?

Our leadership group formulates the team rules. We had a lot of discussion our first year about those. Every August during pre-season practice, I will meet with the group. I will give them a copy of the rules from the previous year, along with a copy of the team goals. Then I will give them a week or so to visit among themselves, and we'll nail all that stuff down together. They do a much better job with making the rules than I ever would. This gives the team some ownership. During the year, we'll remind them that these are the rules the team has chosen- let's make sure we abide by them.

How do you choose your team captains?

As coaches, we'll select individual game captains during the season. At the end of the year, the players will vote on captains, and we announce them at the team banquet. We try to spread the ownership around because we can include underclassmen as well as the seniors when we have different captains each game.

What role do they play in terms of holding their teammates accountable for poor play or bad behavior off the field?

The seniors are asked to serve as our primary leaders. The main thing we want to see from them is setting a great example for others to follow.

Do you prepare the team any differently the week leading up to play a big name opponent like Ohio State? If not, what do you see as the most important factors in weekly game preparation in general?

The so-called "big games" that everyone has on their schedule are the easiest games to coach in because everyone knows that this is a big game, so the guys already have that extra motivation and focus.

Our biggest challenge is to coach the week after those "big games," especially after a big win, and we are the favorite in the next game. We try to emphasize the importance of all 11, soon to be 12, games on the schedule. They are all significant. It's not like baseball where you play so many games. When you only have 11 or 12 opportunities, they are all critical. That old adage about not being able to get up every week is ridiculous. Every player should be ready for all the games. We want to have a consistency in the way we do things.

What are your thoughts on pep talks?

You want to be careful about riding an emotional roller coaster. For every peak, there is a valley and that can be dangerous. Pre-game is really more about reminders. We want to go over the key focus points for our players.

It might be an area of the kicking game that we are really focusing on for the next opponent. It could be a few points offensively or defensively that are going to be key for us if we are going to have success.

Starting on Tuesdays we begin going over things we think are critical for the upcoming game. Friday night I will go over the most important items we've talked about during the week. Saturday is just review. There is a lot of repetition here.

A team that is too tight or over-eager can be a big a problem as any. What do you say when you can tell the team is overly emotional?

That's tough because I'm not really a good joke teller. We try to work in some pre-game remarks that emphasize going out and playing our game and not worrying about the circumstances.

- 14 -

BILLY DONOVAN: INDIVIDUAL VERSUS TEAM MOTIVATION

University of Florida basketball coach Billy Donovan has led the Gators to two national titles and three Final Four appearances.

One of Billy Donovan's favorite books is "The Precious Present," by Spencer Johnson. It takes little effort to figure out the book's moral- that living in the moment is the key to happiness. It takes considerably more to do as Donovan has done and live that message every day. He asks his players to forget the last game and not look to the future. Can they live in the present?

"It is wise for me to think about the past and to learn from my past. But it is not wise for me to be in the past. For that is how I lose myself." Quote from The Precious Present.

Two weeks into his tenure at Florida, Donovan told his assistant coaches, "I think we can win a national championship here."

Taking that outlook 15 seasons ago was ambitious. It meant taking a mediocre program to the sport's highest level. Donovan started by recruiting quality players with reputations as hard workers and persuaded them to come build something. A run to the national title game followed in 2000.

In 2006 and 2007, he achieved the dream with back-to-back national titles. Then came a few down seasons with no NCAA births. His "live in the moment" mentality kept them from dwelling on the disappointment of those NIT years. The Gators learned to focus on each day and not what had happened before.

"My past was present. And my future will be present. The present moment is the only reality I ever experience." Quote from The Precious Present.

Depending on whom you ask, Donovan's success comes back to one of a few things- his work ethic, his focus on the mental aspect of the game and his ability to recruit and motivate players.

Athletic Director Jeremy Foley said Donovan's work ethic hasn't changed. Each day demands complete focus on the task at hand. "Right now" has become his catchphrase for the year, and players give a knowing smile when asked how much Donovan focuses on that.

"He says that almost every day, in practice and games," said senior center Vernon Macklin. "And it's the truth. We must live in the moment. We can't think about the past, can't live in the future."

In the offseason, Donovan seeks feedback from other coaches. He never feels like he has it figured out, and makes sure his players know they don't either.

"He always wants to undress what we're doing and see if he can find another way, or find a crack and remove a weakness," said assistant coach Larry Shyatt.

All the while, Donovan is equal parts psychologist and motivator. Ask him about why his team struggled in a win, and he's more likely to give an answer about why his players didn't handle the "human element" than why they struggled against a 2-3 zone.

What did you learn from former University of Kentucky and current Boston Celtic coach Rick Pitino (whom Donovan played for at Providence)?

"He wanted feedback constantly, and he created chemistry. He squashed egos and got guys to buy into the team and his system. Coach Pitino took an active interest in my life away from basketball. I always felt like he cared. I don't want any of our players to ever think that I don't care. If they think I don't care, then I've done a poor job spending time with them away from the practice court. There are things going on socially, academically and in the basketball world, that can prevent them from playing up to their ability, so knowing them as a total person helps with motivation."

Discuss some general thoughts on motivation.

"It's our job as coaches to find out how each player is motivated, what makes them tick and obviously try to go about handling them the best way we can to get them to fulfill their obligation to the team. There are some guys I have to bring in the office and talk to them one-on-one, others need to be brought out into the crowd.

When you're dealing with a team, I don't think you can just say this is the way we're going to do things. I've got to try and find ways to get each guy to fulfill their responsibility by understanding who that person is as an individual."

Times have changed. When I was playing in high school and college, there was a separation. I never dreamed about going into a coach's office, sitting down and shooting the breeze. You just didn't do that. Maybe there are certain coaches who still try to keep themselves at that distance level, who don't want to get too close to the players.

I have no problem with a kid coming in here, joking around with him and having a good time with him away from the court. I want players to feel good about themselves, and to know me, and for the bond to be something that after they leave here, there is a relationship beyond player/coach, to consider me someone that will be there for them. At the same time, I'm not going to tolerate anything less than those kids giving me their best every day."

In the off-season as he put the players through their paces, strength and conditioning coach Scott Webster wore a Gonzaga Basketball t-shirt as a daily reminder of who knocked Florida out of the 1999 tournament.

Do you think it is productive to remind a team of a past failure to moti-vate?

"Coach Webster came in and checked to see if he could do it. I told him I had no problem with it. I think we needed to be reminded of that game. You want that in the back of their mind as they're working out. Those guys got a little taste of the NCAA Tournament last year. So you want to remember Gonzaga, not to dwell on it, but to understand through past mistakes, this is what we've got to do to put ourselves in a better position. Hopefully that game motivated us this year (the team reached the NCAA final in 2000).

You have been brought in an array of sensational talent. How do you keep all these heralded prep stars content? How do you establish team harmony and unity and get kids to accept their role?

"Everybody needs to be treated fairly. Everybody needs to be treated the same. We have certain rules on our team and if those rules are bro-ken, regardless of whether you're the leading scorer or the last guy on the bench, you're going to be treated the same way. However, you have to realize you're dealing with a lot of different entities, a lot of differ-ent individuals, therefore each individual is motivated and plays the game of basketball for different reasons.

If I look at it, as everybody's the same, every personality's the same, that's where you run into trouble, and you probably aren't maximizing coaching that young man if you take the personality out of it. You have to understand you're dealing with 11 entirely different people, and everybody's motivated differently.

Our freshmen came in and were very, very humble. They gave our upperclassmen a lot of respect, and I thought those two ingredients gave our team very good chemistry. Our guys put winning as the most important thing. The combination of unselfishness and guys under-standing their roles- that's why we won. That's the important thing to me, guys putting winning first and foremost."

The team concept was equally embraced by the youngsters.

"If people were worried about individual statistics, they wouldn't come to Florida," said one former player. "We play too many guys, we're not going to put up big numbers- nobody on our team is going to lead the SEC in scoring, assists or rebounds because each player doesn't play enough."

Earlier in the season, highly touted freshman Brett Nelson started to play like he was out there all by himself. In high school, Nelson knew if he didn't take control of a game, it didn't get done. But he got over that and started to blend in nicely with the team.

"My whole thing is winning, whether I play two minutes or 40 minutes," said Nelson. "The main thing about this system is that it's very unselfish. We try to make the extra pass and make our teammates better."

Now that Florida basketball reached new highs, how does the team deal with expectations?

"You want the bar to be raised. I don't get that concerned about expectations among media people and fans. I'm more concerned with expectations of myself and the expectations of the coaches on ourselves and our kids. And when you can talk about being the best, that's good.

I wish that during my first year at Florida, there were more expectations placed on our basketball team. That first year team felt they weren't supposed to win, especially against top ranked teams like Kentucky or Arkansas. That's the difference between top-notch programs like Kentucky, Duke, and Kansas and everybody else. They expect to win- they expect to be there every game.

There wasn't much I could do about the situation. I could sit and look 'em in the face and tell 'em they could win, but I don't think they'd believe it. Winning makes guys understand everything they're going through, there's a purpose and a method behind the scheme. The pre-season conditioning, the practices, and the amount of time that's put in is for winning. Certainly once you have some success; it builds confidence within the team, and creates an excitement and enthusiasm level.

What are your thoughts on recruiting?

"A lot of times kids get recruited mostly by the assistant coaches, so they never really get to know the head coach in the process. I've taken a different approach. I try to recruit like when I was an assistant coach at Kentucky. It's more hands-on."

The preceding interview was compiled from various sources including the Orlando Sentinel and Gainesville Sun newspapers and Gatorbait magazine.

- 15 -

JOEL SOUTHERN: BALANCING ATHLETIC AND ACADEMIC RESPONSIBILITIES

Joel Southern is the Head Baseball Coach and an Adjunct Chemistry Professor at Elmhurst College.

Let's say you have an athlete who is extremely self-motivated concerning athletics, but doesn't have that same passion for schoolwork. Are there any ways to get him to transfer that same drive into academic pursuits?

I don't believe you can be committed to excellence in one area and not committed to excellence in another. That is going to show up somewhere. If you are willing to cut corners or not finish the job when it comes to schoolwork, it will eventually manifest itself in other areas as well. The athlete may think they are completely committed to what they are doing from an athletic standpoint, but eventually it will catch up to them.

I'm a faculty member in the chemistry department. Our other coaches have advanced degrees, so we can serve as a model to the student-athletes. The "too cool for school" mentality that says you are a nerd if you do well in class can run rampant among athletes. We have to fight against that. I reject the idea that you can't be excellent in more than one thing.

What do you say when you can sense that a player isn't really pushing themselves academically?

The main overarching thing is to emphasize the importance of academics on a daily basis. Two of the big buzz phrases in baseball these days are "play disciplined" and "on-base percentage." So if you want those things to happen, you have to emphasize how important they are. You talk about it every day. Then it becomes part of how they go about their business.

We don't just talk about their academic performance, we monitor it as well. We have study halls. Since our coaching staff members are also faculty members, we can step in and say to their teachers, "Hey, we are really serious about these guys going to class. We need to know if a kid is in trouble or having an issue."

My off-field responsibility is to monitor our guys' academic progress. If a kid is doing poorly in one class, we will ask them what they are doing to change the situation. I tell the kids, "Hey, this is a small school. One of the great things we have here is the ability to meet one-on-one with your professors. You can find a tutor fairly easily."

Specifically, we look at grades, and we ask them what they are doing to improve.

If they say something vague like, "I'll do better," I will ask what behaviors they are going to change to accomplish that. They need to answer what they plan to start doing differently to improve. It takes a lot of follow up to see where they are and how things are progressing. You can't just say, "Study hard, and take care of your academics." and be done with it.

We try to lead the horse to water so to speak. We don't follow them back to their dorm room. There is a fine line with being too invasive and giving them too much freedom. These guys need to learn on their own how to take care of their business.

We as coaches do have the ultimate leverage of playing time. We don't tell them, "Hey, if you don't get a 3.0 you won't play," but if the academics slip and they need a re-fresher for why they are here, we'll sit them down.

What is your role in helping athletes develop more disciplined study habits? How can you help athletes become better time managers?

As soon as they get on campus, players are in a structured environment. They have fall workouts and we start our weight-lifting program at that time. We start study halls for the freshman in the second week. Sophomore and juniors whose GPAs may be trending in the wrong direction may be in those study halls as well (they are held twice a week).

Let's say an athlete doesn't have a class until 11 am- it becomes real easy to sleep in. We want them to develop more disciplined study habits, so we may suggest a 9 am study hall. We want them out of bed and letting them know what they should be doing- whether it's at study hall or working from the dorm. They should be looking over notes, working on project assignments, etc. Some guys come out of high school without having to do much homework or without having to manage their time. We are replacing the parents in the sense of monitoring what they are doing in class.

We do "spot checks" to see if they are attending class. We don't want to mass email professors and ask them who is and who isn't attending, so periodically we check for ourselves. We want our guys to sit in the first 3 rows of class all year. Our reasoning is simple- it's easy to sit in the first 3 rows when they first get here in September, but then when the 12th week of the semester rolls around, the kids will have a tendency to zone out. You are more likely to pay better attention in the front of class. It's a preemptive strike. This will cause you to have better class habits.

If people aren't making proper use of their study hall, showing up unprepared, or if they are late to class, I'll have to hammer them on that. The whole coaching staff and myself are big believers on team consequences for individual mess-ups. If one kid gets in trouble on campus or continually misses classes, it effects us all. That's something that especially the freshmen have to understand.

Another thing we do as far as monitoring is give the players calendars. We tell them that they need to write out for the next couple of weeks what projects are due when, the dates of any presentation you have to give, and any upcoming exam dates. At least once a week, I will look at those calendars and say, "Ok, you have a paper due next Wednesday, is it completed? What have you done for that so far? Where are you in the process?"

Lots of times assignments are given at the start of the semester, but they need a little prompting to get going. Being a good student involves planning your time. Telling them, "hey, you can start working on that right now so it won't overwhelm you at the last minute" is an important concept to reinforce.

This comes back to getting them to form good habits. We tell them, "You can plan ahead. You can use your calendar. When something is done, mark it off." That way, they can chart their own progress along the way.

It gets very difficult in the spring during baseball season, when there are more temptations to blow off academics. Let's say practice is at 2 pm, and there is a home game later that night. It's easy for a student to sleep in until 11, grab lunch and then head over to batting practice. We really have to fight that. I tell the guys, "Look, we're not professionals. We don't have the option of phoning in the rest of our day and just showing up at the ball park."

On the other hand, we're not running an intramural team here. We're 64-23 the last two seasons. I like to think winning that many games is a by-product of the way we are going about our business. By focusing more on process than winning, we end up doing very well.

Based on your job as both teacher and coach, what success principles translate best for both academics and athletics?

As a teacher, I don't have the same leverage I have as a coach writing out a line-up card. It's a big motivator in dictating performance- who plays and who doesn't.

At the Division 3 level (non-scholarship), you are more likely to see a co-curricular emphasis between academics and athletics. We sell that to our prospective student-athletes. You get some players who think they can "turn it on and turn it off" when it comes to academics. I don't buy that. We talk about commitment to excellence in all areas. That doesn't mean we expect everyone to have a 4.0 GPA, but we do expect them to work up to their abilities.

As a coach, you can have so much more of an effect on the students than as a teacher. If non-athlete students don't want to apply themselves, there is not a lot a teacher can do. However, athletics is the ultimate meritocracy. If you can't get the job done, we'll find someone else who will or try a different approach.

My coaching philosophy permeates how I teach. I talk about hard work, discipline, accountability, finishing the job you start, and sacrificing current comfort for future gain. I challenge some of the students to get up to speed. In the classroom, the student will often turn it around and think it is the teacher's fault if they do poorly. So the coaching principles don't always work as well in the classroom.

I think that when a coach emphasizes academics, it means so much more to a player than hearing it from a teacher. It's expected from a teacher, but not necessarily from a coach.

- 16 -

GAIL GOESTENKORS: MOTIVATIONAL TOOL BOX FOR A SUCCESSFUL PROGRAM

Texas Women's Basketball coach Gail Goestenkors has led her teams to 17 consecutive NCAA tournament appearances, including four Final 4s with Duke.

What psychological aspects of coaching do you consider most important, and why?

Understanding that each player is motivated differently. To accomplish that, you have to get to know the player and find out what's important to them. Some players need to be yelled at, while others will shut down under the same treatment. Finding that balance is key. The team must also understand that we each have different personalities, and we are motivated differently. They need to know that I will push individuals in different ways for the good of the team.

I read an article that said you have put together highlight films of the team's best moments as a motivational tool. Are there any other creative ways you have found to motivate your team in the past?

When we played a regular season game at Georgia Tech, I took the team to the Georgia Dome (site of the Women's Final 4). Our theme last year was "One Team, One Dream." We went inside the Dome and I told them to get comfortable with the surroundings. We had five freshmen on the team who I wanted especially to see what it was like. I talked about the dream and what it would take to make it happen.

If an athlete gets into a shooting slump, but her technical form is fine, what would you say to that player to help her recover?

First, I would give them more personal attention. I would start to shoot with them. I would give positive reinforcement like, "Don't worry-you are a great shooter." while I'm shooting with her. I would play some fun shooting games like horse, where they can relax and not think too much about their slump. This way they won't stress out as much about their shot. Generally, if the form is fine, but you struggle, confidence is an issue. The game then becomes stressful. I want the game to become fun again. They usually get their confidence back because they can beat me. Then we'll put together a highlight tape of them making shot after shot. That will help them regain their confidence and touch of when they were shooting well.

Are there any particular team-building exercises you have used that have been consistently beneficial to your team over the years?

When they get back from summer, we do show and tell- just like you did in kindergarten. Everybody has to bring something from home that means something to them and something that the team doesn't necessarily know about. Five minutes before each practice session, we have a different player do her show and tell. This brings the team closer together. They're sharing themselves and their childhood with each other. It's also nerve-wracking for the freshman when they get up there for the first time. It gives the rest of the team empathy because they've all been in that situation where you're speaking in front of the team for the first time, and you're sharing part of yourself with them.

We have them do book reports. Players have to stand up in front of their teammates and kind of put themselves out there and talk about what they have learned through the book. I probably have about thirty books that we have used over the last couple of years.

Are they mostly sports related or about any subject?

Anything, but mostly sports related. "It's Not About the Bike," by Lance Armstrong is one of my favorites. There are basketball books like "A Season is a Lifetime" by Duke Men's Coach K and "Values of the Game" by Bill Bradley which are great.

Short books like "Who Moved My Cheese?" or "The Precious Present" can be read very quickly. In cases like that, I'll assign them two books. We assign the books to players depending on what we think they need to hear.

For instance we gave "Who Moved My Cheese?" to a freshman because she was very rigid in her ways. She needed to become more flexible and understand that there are other ways to do things. It was good because after she read it, she said, "Okay, now I get it." She knew exactly what I was trying to get at with her. Since we've read all the books and know the themes, we sit down as a staff and decide which book will be assigned to which player.

Are there any other exercises you have found that build team unity?

We have a trail around the golf course that we run- it's about three miles. It's good for conditioning because it's very hilly and mentally and physically challenging. We do that run during the preseason, then again during the season at some point. We say, "It doesn't matter how fast you go, it's about team, and we're all going to cross the finish line together." They do the run on their own, and they have to stick together as a group. Everyone stays at the same pace. The run is harder on some than others.

For instance, last year one player really struggled the most with the trail. So the rest of the team said "Okay, you (the player) are going to lead us, and we're going to follow." They knew the only rule I had was that they all had to come in together at the same time. It didn't matter how fast or slow they were. So the player who usually struggled ran her best time because she wanted to lead the team.

When you first came to Duke, the resources aren't anything like you have today. What advice would you say to a coach who is trying to build a program with limited resources?

Work ethic is essential, because you have a lot of ground to make up. You must do things the right way. There are no short cuts. Never lose your integrity. Regardless of resources, the personal touch is always most important. Don't be afraid to be creative.

How do you help an athlete balance all their academic and athletic responsibilities while they are in your program?

We start off with eight hours of required study hall for all freshmen. The freshman year in particular is a tough adjustment, so learning time management skills are very important. The eight hours of study hall is held in the academic center- just one floor down from my office, so it's perfect because we're in the same building. There is someone in charge, and the players have to sign in and out. There are tutors in the study hall room to meet with players if they need it.

I have two coaches that are in charge of the academics. They both oversee a couple of players. The kids have to turn in their grades every week. The two coaches have a copy of their syllabi so they know when they have a paper due and can ask, okay, "where's the first draft, where's the second draft-" those kind of things. Especially here, the academics are difficult so we know we need to make sure they start off well to help their academic confidence level.

Do you give them any time management training at all?

They have someone that comes in and speaks to them early on about time management, about test taking, and those kinds of issues. There are so many resources available. During the first month they have at least one meeting a week with someone who is here to try and help them.

When you're talking to a student who is feeling pressured and stressed out, what advice do you give them?

When they are feeling overwhelmed, we tell them to write down everything that they are doing within a day. Find out where they are wasting time and where they can be more productive. Instead of coming over to Cameron (the training facility) on three different occasions, let's get you over here once to do your practice, your study hall and your weight lifting all at the same time as opposed to three different trips. Usually you can find some time that's been wasted. Watching Jerry Springer in the afternoon is not real productive. (Laughs)

Can you discuss staff relationships and keeping productivity high?

Every year we change responsibilities which helps coaches not get too comfortable or get in a rut. A different coach is in charge of recruiting each year. I have coaches move up with a class- that helps with relationship building. I also want my assistants to become head coaches if they desire. I need to help them become very well rounded. We all share scouting responsibilities. I make sure they don't scout the same teams each year.

What are the most important elements of being a successful recruiter? Are there any "sales strategies" that get prospects excited during official campus and home visits?

We're very genuine with the recruits. We don't try to make things better than they are. I always try to speak from the heart when I talk to players. I don't tell them what they want to hear, but I am truthful with them. Kids can tell if you are just 'blowing smoke," so be honest.

How about strategic aspects of recruiting?

We meet every week as a staff and decide who is going to call what prospect for the upcoming week. I'll call every other week and have one of my assistants call in the off week because I want them to get to know the entire staff. They need to get to know me best since I will be making the decisions once they get here.

Besides being academically and athletically talented, what evaluation criteria do you use to evaluate high school prospects?

Besides talent, work ethic and attitude are very important. We learn about the prospects by talking with them, their parents, and their coaches. Checking out what kind of relationship they have with their parents and coaches is important. We talk with the school guidance counselors as well to see if they will be able to handle the academic responsibilities.

- 17 -

GEORGE HORTON: TURNING AROUND A SEASON ON THE BRINK

George Horton is the Head Baseball Coach at the University of Oregon. He was formerly with Cal State Fullerton where he led the Titans to the 2004 NCAA Championship and was named the 2003 and 2004 American Baseball Coaches Association National Coach of The Year.

What mental toughness techniques or exercises had the most impact on the players during last season?

The biggest thing was to change their perspective. In the middle of the season we had gone to Austin, Texas and got swept by the Longhorns, and it was not even close. The energy on the team was as low as I have ever seen it- I think that the staff and players were thinking that this was a rebuilding year and that we were going to struggle.

Sport Psychologist Ken Ravizza came in and talked to the team and the first thing he asked was, "What were we doing well?" We were playing good defense, and up to that point, I think we were all focusing on the negatives. The next thing he told us was that we had an opportunity to do what no Titans team had ever done before.

Most of our guys were thinking, "Yeah, be the first Titans team to go unranked for a long time," but what he said was, "be the first Titan team to go from under .500 at the middle of the season, to being National Champions." That really caught our guys' attention.

He then asked our guys to, "Think how good it is going to feel" when you get to Omaha. From that point on, you could really see a weight lifted off of our guy's backs. P.J. Pillitere, one of our veteran players would write that saying, "Think how good it is going to feel" on the dugout wall. Our guys rallied around that saying.

At the middle point of our season we were all caught up in the results and since we were not getting the results we wanted, we started to press. In baseball you have no control over the results- all you can do is play one pitch at a time and work the process. We all got back to the process, quality at-bats, quality pitches and playing the game one pitch at a time. I think that helped turn it around for us.

Talk about the year you made the amazing comeback to win the NCAA tournament 2 years ago. What factors do you attribute to the turn-around that season?

I think a lot of the stuff that we talked about before, changing the collective perspective, getting back to the process and focusing more on one pitch at a time and controlling what we could control.

I think another factor was that our guys continued to work hard every day. Our staff did a great job of staying on top of the fundamental work that needed to happen every day with our guys for them to continue to get better.

We also changed our coaching perspective and instead of catching our guys doing things wrong, we began catching our players doing things right. I think the whole atmosphere at practice and games was changed because of that subtle change in the way we were dealing with the players.

We had a very special group of Titans that year, and I think that their chemistry on and off the field also helped us turn it around. They were as close a knit group of guys as I have coached, they all pulled for each other, it did not matter who was at the plate or on the mound. We had all 25 guys pulling in the same direction and when you get that going, special things will happen.

How did you as a coaching staff reinforce those techniques?

Our staff had been intact for a long time. We had always been big believers in the Mental Game, but often got caught up in the day-to-day operations of a baseball program and sometimes did not reinforce or talk about the Mental Game as much as we probably could or should have. In 2004, we really made a conscious effort to reinforce the techniques that Ken emphasized.

We would spend more time talking about each of our player's routines and the importance of taking that good deep breath as the pitcher gets set, or as the hitter gets into the batters box. I think as a staff we also did a better job of letting go of the negatives and getting back to the next pitch. As a coach you need to model what you want your players to be doing. I think that is the best type of reinforcement.

Do you ever change the way you are preparing a team during the season if things aren't going as planned?

We spend a lot of time preparing for the unexpected. We will often have umpires make bad calls on purpose in scrimmages so that we can see how our guys will respond, but most importantly, so that we can teach our guys how we want them to respond.

If things are not going as planned, we will make some changes. The key to peak performance and sustaining success is being able to compensate and adjust- it is not about being perfect. Perfection is like a double-edged sword, while it motivates you to do better, it is also the constant critic and no matter what you do, it is never good enough.

Many of the guys that we get have never really failed before. These were all the best players in high school and when they get here they realize that the game has sped up for them, that they are now playing at a different level. We often have to slow things down a bit if we have a younger team vs. getting more into the intricate details of the game if we have more veteran players who have been a part of the system at Fullerton for a few years.

The will to win- is it inherent in a player, or are there things you can do as a coach to bring that desire out of an individual?

That is a great question, a question that I often think about and discuss with my colleagues. For the majority of guys playing Division I

Baseball, motivation is not a problem because they have had to work very hard to get to that level. I think that the will to win is important, but the will to prepare is VITAL.

I think that our guys prepare and practice so hard that they feel they deserve to win every time they step on the field. I think that the previous Titans were able to establish a level of competitiveness and excellence that brings out the best in our current guys.

We are constantly looking for ways to motivate our guys, but we have found that the best way is pure competition. Whether it is in the weight room or an intra-squad scrimmage, our guys want to compete and want to win.

What advice would you give to the young coaches reading this book?

The best place to start is to find a person who can be a mentor for you, a person who is in a position or a place that you would like to go. I have been blessed to have worked with and alongside some of the best minds in baseball- Augie Garrido, Dave Snow, Wally Kincaid, Ben Hines, Rick Vanderhook, Dave Serrano and Ken Ravizza are just a few.

Attend coaching clinics, and become a student of the game. I learn something new about the game or about a way to run my program each and every day. That is what makes baseball and coaching so much fun- realizing that you will never know everything about the game and the profession. My motivation is knowing that I have the chance to learn something new and pursue getting better each and every day.

What factors do you attribute to the consistent level of success at your program?

I think there are a lot of factors that contribute to the levels of success that Cal State Fullerton Baseball has been able to achieve. It all started well before I got here with the previous Titans setting the bar for excellence. There is a lot of pride and tradition in being able to wear Titans across your chest. Every time our guys suit up to go play, we remind them that they represent not only themselves and the team, but all the former Titans that have gone through our program.

I think our guys work as hard day in and day out as anyone in the country. We take a lot of pride in getting better every day. We also work very hard on the fundamentals. We emphasize the little things every day. Bunting, base running, execution- those types of things that we rely so heavily on in games, we must do in practice every day.

We also try to make our practices as game-like as possible. When we scrimmage, we often start with runners on base and use the scoreboard to make the game more realistic. We also are able to recruit great talent, and that helps to make our intra-squads all that much more competitive because you have to compete every day to win a position.

Once you have climbed to the peak, how do you challenge a team to maintain that level of excellence?

We challenge our guys the same way whether we are coming off a National Championship season or a season in which we finished short of our goals. The challenge is to get better every day and to have quality at-bats and throw quality pitches. That is all you can control in baseball, and that is what we want our players to strive for consistently.

In baseball there is a lot of failure. If you focus on the results and lose sight of the process, you will find yourself carrying the weight of the world and not playing up to your potential.

The challenge is to play the game the right way each pitch. That is a lot easier said then done, but it is something that we work on every single day. The team that wins the most pitches is usually the team that wins the game. We focus on the details and doing the little things- that is the level of excellence that the previous Titans have set and the level that we strive for every season.

What traits did your championship teams possess that helped them become champions?

The common traits that our best teams have had are a discipline and a desire to get better every day and to work on the fundamentals of the game. Our championship teams, like many of our teams that fall short of that goal get after it every day and compete with each other to get better.

I think there was a confidence and a belief that they could be champions. Our championship teams also played the game one pitch at a time and focused on the things that they could control. There was not a lot of talk about the draft and things that were out of their control, simply getting better every day and controlling what we can control.

Is there any benefit to a pep talk speech before a game?

I am not a big believer in big pep talks before games because I think it can get guys overly emotional and too excited. At our level, success is all about consistency and doing what you do on a daily basis in practice in games. That is why our practice time is so important.

We want our guys to play at their pace and to treat every game like a practice, and every practice like a game so that nothing changes. Our goal is to play Titan Baseball and let everything else take care of itself. We are going to throw strikes, play catch and put the ball in play. If we can do that with a focus on the process, in the present moment with a positive mindset, we are giving ourselves the best chance to be successful.

If anything, I think I try to get our guys to relax before a game because they are often excited for the game and can easily get too excited and play out of character if they get caught up in the results and the pressures of playing in a big game vs. doing what they do on a daily basis.

Interview by Brian Cain, Performance Coach www.briancain.com

- 18 -

Ross Fichtner: Character Coaching Builds Performance On and Off the Field

Ross Fichtner is a former All-Pro defensive back coach with the Green Bay Packers and the Cleveland Browns. He developed the character-coaching program for his work with the Fellowship of Christian Athletes (FCA).

Could you discuss the importance of building character qualities in athletes, and how a coach can accomplish this?

An FCA survey of 10,000 athletes revealed that 92 percent of respondents said that a coach- for good or bad- was the most influential person in their lives.

Coaches have a great opportunity to positively impact an athlete's life. So why not build character traits into their lives that they can carry with them forever. Teaching character qualities can be difficult. The first step is that you must display them yourself.

The key is to work on getting character qualities built into practice routines, by asking athletes certain questions that relate to character. Each coach has to come up with what works best for them when incorporating character traits into their training routines.

Once athletes know the definition of a character quality, and they get praised or criticized based on whether or not they exhibit that character quality, they start to realize, "Hey, I'm making the coach happy when I'm attentive, and my performance improves."

As you build in character with your coaching, you will see step-by-step improvements. Your kids may only develop a certain level of attentiveness or dependability that helps on the field, but these are also qualities they will take with them long after their sport careers are over. After being drilled on character issues time and time again, players will start to display these qualities.

Character won't help an athlete jump higher or run faster, but when you have athletes with character, all the close games that could go either way will usually go to the team with better or more character.

One quick example: Thoroughness is a character quality that is really lacking in today's society. Carrying out all the details and doing the little things, instead of a halfway job is really important. Doing so will help an athlete improve his/her life off the field as well.

Could you cite a specific example of how a player learned a character quality that made a difference in their athletic performance?

A friend took over as a quarterback coach at Wheaton College. During the previous year, their QB led the country in interceptions. Looking at film, the coach immediately saw that the quarterback was not decisive. Arm strength wasn't a problem, but he threw into coverage and didn't take the right reads. The coach developed a series of drills to get the player to be more decisive.

One drill was to have a stop watch and allow no more than 3 seconds to pass the ball. If he didn't, the whistle would blow.

The coach would also take the quarterback to a chalkboard and ask him to draw up a certain play. He had to tell the coach exactly where each receiver or running back would be within a few seconds. Based on what the defense was doing, he would decide whom to throw to.

The next season, the same QB threw over 600 passes with only 3 interceptions.

The key character quality here was decisiveness. Many years later this same young man worked for a company where he was described as the most decisive leader in the whole organization.

Talk about the importance of having rules or a set of standards to live by for a team.

I visited a college who had two players miss practice the day before the game. They were taking a make up test that they could have taken any day of the week. They didn't bother to tell the coach.

I met with the coach on game day, and he lamented the fact that the kids didn't follow instructions and missed practice. I asked him what he was going to do. He said, "I'm going to let them play. We really need them for the game."

I asked him what team rules covered this kind of thing. He said, "I don't believe in rules."

I told him he would always be in trouble with that philosophy. You are going to be wrong no matter what. If you bring them back with no consequences, you have, in effect, told the rest of the team "I can cut practice anytime, and it's no big deal."

If you don't let them play, you are hurting the team's chance for victory.

But when you have set rules, the coach is never the bad guy. All you have to do is enforce the rules. If you had a set rule against missing practice, you could say, "Hey, you let your teammates down by skipping practice. Here are the consequences that you already knew about." It may be missing the game or extra stair step running at 6 a.m. It takes the pressure off the head coach.

It seem that people have an excuse for everything these days, and very few people have to pay the price for disobedience. They expect to get away with anything. Lessons are great for character building.

Discuss the keys to being a great leader.

A friend of mine went to the Naval Academy. On the first day of a class on leadership, the professor asked them to break up into groups of five, and pick one great leader throughout history. There were three common qualities that each displayed: 1) They had a positive image of themselves, and they knew where they wanted to go. 2) They knew whom they represented. 3) They inspired people to follow them.

Many people who never become great leaders can't see themselves as leaders. It's an image problem.

Are leaders born, or can they be developed?

It's difficult to develop a leader, but it can be done. They must develop those three qualities described above. They can look at a situation and say, "we're here now, but here is where we want to be. This is what we have to do to get there."

True greatness is not a goal one sets out to do; instead it is a byproduct of learning how to serve others. A great leader would not focus on the power, but submit to a higher authority and look to serve others.

Discuss the desire for immediate fulfillment vs. desire for lasting achievement in the context of a coach taking over a new program that has not had much success in the past.

Let's say a coach takes over a run down program. He or she can't expect an immediate turnaround. They need to look down the road and work on a vision that could take five years or more. Once developed, you must sell the team on the vision.

The first step is to have a one-to-one meeting with players and ask them point blank, "What are your goals and expectations?" Make sure the goals you all come up with are believable, achievable and accountable, and then hold them to it. Ask them, "What steps are you going to take individually to see us achieve our goals, and what can I do to help?"

Here are 10 character qualities by definition and questions you should ask your players to make sure they are displaying them.

1) Alertness- Being aware of the events taking place around me so that I can have the right responses to them:

    A. Does the athlete see game situations developing, or does to coach have to alert him or her?

    B. Does the athlete know who is in the game both for his/her team and the opponents?

    C. Does the athlete hear and see the communications from teammates and coaches?

    D. Does the athlete always know the time and situation of the game?

2) Boldness- Demonstrating the confidence that doing what is right will bring ultimate victory regardless of present opposition:

    A. Does the athlete speak up when they see a wrong being done?

    B. Does the athlete jump into a game plan without hesitation?

    C. Does the athlete fear being rejected on the basis of convictions?

3) Courage- Fulfilling my responsibilities in spite of being afraid:

    A. Does a fear of getting injured prevent the athlete from giving 100% all the time?

    B. Can the athlete play hard, even while hurting?

    C. Does the athlete remain silent or speak the truth, even when it's unpopular?

4) Determination- Purposing to accomplish goals on time regardless of the opposition:

    A. Does the athlete always finish an assignment that a coach gives?

    B. Does the athlete allow distractions to hinder him/her in completing an assignment?

    C. Has the athlete ever quit because he/she thought that winning was improbable?

    D. Can the athlete overcome obstacles to achieve goals?

5) Enthusiasm- Learning what actions and attitudes please teammates and coaching staff and getting excited to do them:

    A. Does the athlete see positive aspects of negative situations?

    B. Does the athlete get excited to play a really tough opponent?

C. Does the athlete's work habits convince coaches that s/he is happy with his/her role on the team?

D. Is the athlete excited about practice?

6) Initiative- Recognizing and doing what needs to be done before being asked to do it:

A. Does the athlete wait to be told to do something even when s/he knows it needs to be done?

B. Does the athlete work on the weak points of his/her game, or does the coach have to tell the athlete what to work on?

C. Does the athlete make the first move to get to know newer teammates?

D. Does the athlete spend extra time studying the game plan?

7) Loyalty- Using difficult times to demonstrate my commitment to others:

A. Does the athlete second-guess coaching decisions on a regular basis?

B. Is the athlete happy for another teammate, even if the team mate gets more credit than s/he deserves?

C. Would the athlete stand up for a teammate even if it would cost him/her something (recognition, playing time, etc)?

D. Does the athlete talk to media about what should stay in the locker room or go public with private issues between team mates?

8) Obedience- Fulfilling instructions so that the one I am serving will be fully satisfied and pleased:

A. Does the athlete break training rules?

B. Do coaches see the athlete make sacrifices for the good of the team?

C. Does the athlete carry out his/her assignments exactly as the coaches ask?

D. Does the athlete comply with school rules and academic requirements?

9) Punctuality- Showing respect for other people and the limited time they have:

    A. Does the athlete arrive to meetings and practices on time?

    B. Does the athlete allow for extra time to plan where s/he needs to be to make sure s/he is not late?

    C. Does the athlete get caught in situations where s/he is rushing in order to be on time?

10) Thoroughness- Realizing that each of our tasks will be reviewed.

    A. When given an assignment, does the athlete carry it out in detail, or does the athlete do just enough to get by?

    B. Does the athlete finish a task before starting another?

    C. Does the athlete turn in assignments without checking accuracy?

- 19 -

TOMMY LIMBAUGH: RECRUITING THE BEST TO YOUR PROGRAM

Tommy Limbaugh is a former 21-year Division 1 assistant football coach who runs recruiting seminars for college coaches.

What are some general traits of successful recruiters?

Part of it is hard work combined with luck. You must have a good system in place so kids will believe in what you are doing.

Assuming you are already a good evaluator of talent, you have to be able to create trust with the recruit and the decision makers. More often than not, it is the mother; so developing a relationship with the primary decision makers where you can create trust is key. The last week to ten days is crunch time for the undecided. Many times where they decide go will come back to whom they trust. It's also important to maintain your credibility throughout the whole process.

How can that trust be developed?

Be your best self. Here is a quick example. When calling a recruit and the parent or sibling answers the phone, don't quickly ask to speak to John or Mary- take a few minutes to talk to the parents. You ask whatever questions you want to ask of them, share what you want to, and just totally include them in the process. I have seen recruiters that would just not include the parents enough. That is a huge mistake. Just assume that everybody you talk to is important in the recruiting process because you never know.

What else can coaches do to influence the recruit?

You need to dare to be different and not sound like everyone else. Don't say the same things that everyone else is saying. There should be a depth to your conviction. People are more influenced by the depth of your conviction than by the height of your logic. When you so deeply believe in your program and your school, athletes feel that conviction. You can't fool people in the long run. They know whether you are being real or not.

What is important is that you work within a context of your own personality; don't try and be somebody you are not. Kids see through that, and parents are even quicker to see through phoniness.

Coaches need to learn the skill of how to close the deal. I think there are certain techniques in learning to close the deal that are very important. You may be great at everything from phone calls to letter-writing to home and official visits. You have created a great relationship, but if you can't close the deal, then everything else is wasted. All these skills are an important part of the process. Closing the deal is a skill that is lacking by a number of coaches. Keep this in mind- coaches should be thinking about closing the deal from the beginning to end, from the first time you meet the recruit to the last time you talk to them.

Each coach should utilize their own personality and sharpen those skills. You have to be yourself. Kids can tell if you are phony. You can't brag on your past playing days, because chances are they have never heard of you as a player. They only know you as a coach.

How important is the official visit in the process, and what role do the current players have in this process?

The official visit is very important. You want to create a situation where you are empathetic to the recruit when they come to visit. They want to attend a school where they feel at home and are comfortable. They are influenced a lot by being around your other players, talking to them when they are out on a Friday or Saturday night.

Recruits are going to ask what it's like on to live on campus and attend school. Your current players have a great influence and therefore they become such critical components in the recruiting process, because they are the ones that can make that recruit feel at home. If players a potential recruits meets on a campus visit don't tell him/her what s/he wants to hear, the recruit will not go there.

You always talk to the players. Have a team meeting where you emphasize how important recruiting weekends are. Make sure current players know that they have a job in helping recruit the best players to come to your school. The end result will be one step closer to winning a championship.

Right before a big recruiting weekend is a great time for a pep talk to get your players motivated to understand the importance of these weekends. The goal is to get as motivated for that recruiting weekend as they are for a ballgame. And it is that important, if not more so, because it influences so many other games down the road.

Who are some head coaches who are great recruiters, and why are they successful?

Former Florida State coach Bobby Bowden was as good as there was during the home visit. The assistant coaches have already created so much trust. You combine that with Bowden's fatherly image, and parents just warm up to him too. He represents the laidback approach.

There are also aggressive guys who come in, thinking that their school is the best and tell recruits, "Hey, if you don't take the scholarship offer right now, then you are not right for our place." I don't recommend this approach, but it works for some people.

What can a team do when a coaching change is in the works?

You can have an assistant coach tell recruits, "No coach can promise you they will be here all 4 years. Coaches come and go, but the program remains. Make your decision based on what school is best for you."

How can a coach find the "diamond in the rough" that few others know about?

One year, Alabama was recruiting a kid named Keith Carter, who was the number one linebacker in Florida. Alabama recruited Carter hard, but missed out on him. Instead they took his teammate, who looked to have some potential. Derrick Thomas then became an All-American, and Carter barely ever got any playing time. So keep your eyes open, and someone could fall into your lap.

What are your thoughts on talent evaluation?

This is not an exact science by any means. Even NFL teams miss on first round draft picks. The key is to get as much information as possible. The more information you have, the more accurate your evaluation will be. You can't lock in on just height, weight and speed- you have got to know about the heart of the youngster and his competitive nature.

You have got to talk to his high school coaches and the people that have been around him and find out those types of intangibles. It's something you can only get through repeated evaluations over the years. I don't know whether you can put it down in a scientific way. It's something you develop a feel for over time.

One physical talent we would always look for is foot quickness. I always started with a player's feet. Regardless of the position in football, every athlete needs to have quick feet.

- 20 -

SUE ENQUIST: INSTILLING THE "GO FOR IT" SPIRIT TO PRODUCE CHAMPIONS

Sue Enquist is the former head coach of UCLA women's softball. First as a player and later as a head coach, she was part of 6 national champion teams.

What factors do you attribute to the consistent level of your success? Once you have climbed to the peak, how do you challenge a team to maintain that level of excellence?

I've been with the UCLA program since the beginning of the program as a player, then as a coach. Over the years, the way players are motivated has changed, but certain things remain the same. The pillars of the program have not changed. Every day you must bring 100% effort and a positive attitude. The next pillar is to have perspective on every day. Succeed in the classroom, make good moral decisions in your social life, and arrive at the field each day by letting go of all the things that may have emptied your emotional well. The third pillar is to match individuals to a profile- we're looking for a certain type of student athlete. The person with a stable foundation who is able to say, "I want to challenge myself in every arena at the highest level." Linking up those 3 pillars, we've been able to sustain excellence even as the culture of sport and motivation changes.

The will to win- is it inherent in a player, or are there things you can do as a coach to bring that desire out of an individual?

The will to win is present in everyone. The challenge is to teach the student-athlete how to unwrap those things that inhibit your will. The most common denominator to inhibit the will is fear. Fear inhibits a player's will to "go for it." Fear inhibits my will to work harder than everyone else because if I do, I will be responsible for the outcome.

The most vulnerable thing an athlete can do is to do everything right. The challenge for athletes in this generation is to be freed up by giving it everything they have. Ultimately, if they lose a game, you win the process. At the end of the day, if you can win the process, the game usually ends up being extremely fun and successful.

At UCLA, there are 3 entities- ourselves, the opponent, and the game. Those 3 factors interact all throughout practice preparation and competition. If I can get my athletes to focus on the game and ourselves, they will learn to love creating that strong will to win each and every day. You don't minimize your opponent- you get educated about them, but they are simply 1 player in this triangle. Other than educating ourselves on their defensive schemes and a pre-set strategy on the pitcher we will face, we don't focus a lot on them.

Do you ever change the way you are preparing a team during the season if things aren't going as planned?

At the core, the first thing is they want to have fun. We know it's not fun if you don't win. Winning and fun go hand in hand. You're not going to have fun and win if you can't physically execute. Our conditioning and training hold up that trampoline of fun and winning. You can sometimes do all the right things and not get the end result so you want. In that case, it's my job to remind the team of the things that they are doing right.

Here's an example: in 2005, we were top 3 in the country at the beginning of the season. We were defending champions, and we ended up playing selfish softball, in my opinion, to start the year. Instead of hitting the ball to the right side and moving runners, we tried to hit home runs and collectively collapsed as a team and dropped to thirteenth.

Never in the history of our program had we dropped so far. But then the team collectively started to see we needed to recover and get back to what made us great which was process-based goals, team goals, and team softball. What does that mean? Having the mindset of purposely wanting to put the ball in play on the right side of the infield or the outfield to advance that runner.

Early on we would get so frustrated and just try to hack our way out of our previous failure of not getting the bunt down. So here's what would happen- in the dugout, I would have lists of goals they could check off. One set of goals was really process-oriented goals. These were goals that we all knew we could accomplish successfully. They didn't even involve the opponent. For example, when you are at bat, the player would take two deep breaths. That has nothing to do with getting a hit or not.

We were able to do things regarding tempo. I wanted them three times in a game to call a timeout and reconvene in the infield when they saw a momentum shift. These were things we could be very good at and then feel good about taking control of our game.

I wanted to change the negative self-talk to positive images. I took all our positive self-talk words and printed them, laminated them and posted them all over the dugout in the last third of the season. I wanted them to see words and say those words in their heads constantly so we could get to the point where we would start being more positive, and start playing team softball.

When we started to do that, we weren't winning right away, but we were playing better. Instead of looking at our team batting average, I wanted them to look at our advancing runner stats. So we began to break our game down into the simplest terms like advancing a runner. So a player could ground out, but did she move a girl from first to second? There are different ways to look at success.

Our team batting average was .250 moving runners from second to third, but our team stat from moving first to second was .390. So I asked them, "Were you putting pressure on yourself?" and "Are you getting overconfident?" I told them not to put a greater value on advancing the runner at second.

So you're telling me you can hit .390 moving her from first to second, but you can only hit .250 from second to third. So what is going on there? Have the same mindset like you are trying to advance the runner from first. They hung on to that philosophy, and it literally carried us through the post-season all the way to the championship game.

What are your views on team rules? Do you set them, or do you allow players to help make them? What are the consequences or penalties for not following them?

We as coaches set and enforce them. We have very few rules- don't lie, don't cheat, don't steal. We ask them to sit in the first 3 rows of class. You can't be late for any meeting, class, game or practice. If you are, you will be suspended from practice or the next game. If it's out of season and they are suspended from practice, they are losing the greatest gift they can give themselves every day. We run a tight ship, but we like to think of it as a fun ship. When there are not a lot of grey areas, everyone understands the rules.

We also have zero tolerance for drugs and alcohol. By placing a high value on ourselves, we try to avoid some of the pressure to compromise when it comes to drugs and alcohol. I know the challenges these athletes face, especially with alcohol. We try to educate them on all levels- whether it is social drinking, binge drinking, or the early stages of functioning alcoholism. All this needs to be discussed so they have the awareness. We're not perfect- our goal is to give them the information and have them digest it so they can have a place to draw from when they need it.

Have you ever done anything from a motivational standpoint that didn't work out as you thought it would?

There are tons of instances when things haven't worked out. Softball is a failure sport, so we are always trying to find new ways to motivate the athletes. There is usually a theme that coaches need to be aware of for any team. There are two types of motivation. A foundation of our program is that the athletes are internally motivated.

Each player must figure out what gets her going every day. We spend time on knowing ourselves and what's important to us. But you can't have just internal motivation. We live in an externally stimulated culture. If you sing the song- "play hard, enjoy the struggle and the satisfaction in knowing you have done your best," you won't get everything you need from your athletes.

When trying to motivate externally, I constantly throw out challenges to the team to see how they will react. Every single day, I put pressure on the team and the individual.

Here is an example: At practice one day, they knew that suicide bunt challenge was on the line. This means that 13 out of the 14 hitters have to put the bunt down. The reward of completing this may be less running or a social event where they do something fun as a group. This day, 12 out of 14 laid the bunt down. Their favorite come back is "double or nothing." We have two specialized runners on the team who do a lot of training on their own within the team. I picked one of them as having to make the bunt.

The team said, "No fair coach." My reply, "The game is not fair. How are you going to handle the situation?"

So the team all gets together with this pinch runner and gives her a quick pep talk on how to get the bunt down. They tell her to use positive self-talk and wait until she is ready for the pitch. This freshman with all the pressure her put down a bunt that could have won a world series game.

After that drill, I asked them what was the lesson learned? Good talent combined with a different attitude can do anything. Good talent is flexible because the season will offer so many different challenges.

That's a motivational drill that worked. There were many similar ones where the team simply didn't get the lesson.

What happens in those times?

I might have changed the rules during an exercise, and they then excuse me of cheating. The lesson I was trying to convey went over their heads and got lost.

So the next week, I will introduce a new motivation to sell the lesson to be learned in a different way or fashion.

Sometimes you have to be honest with your team. When you introduce challenges into your practice routine that don't work, you need to be honest and tell them, "Hey, this didn't work." This shows accountability on the coaches' side- which is also very important.

For example, "Today, we tried drill A B and C. The purpose was to learn such and such lesson. Well, it didn't work. My goal next week is to try things differently that will illustrate the lesson we want you to learn."

This way, they know that we aren't perfect either. The goal is to have a good level of communication with your players without being their best friend.

I tell them, "When you go through those chain link fences, you need to separate the rest of your day from practice. You can escape for 3 hours and have a bundle of fun."

One last thought- you have to enable the athlete to enjoy "going for it." If you can get them so focused on "going for it" and not worrying about the results part, you are on your way to peak performance.

When it gets time to put down that suicide bunt- going for it is the fun part, not whether you pop it up or not. Good talent will take care of the proper mechanics. However, it is fear that inhibits the will and your confidence.

- 21 -

MIKE BELLOTTI:
A TO Z PROGRAM BUILDING

ESPN Analyst Mike Bellotti was the former Head Football Coach of the University of Oregon. He is the school's all-time wins leader.

What is your basic approach to pre-game motivation?

As a coach, a lot of times, what is in your mind as the biggest game and a must win, is something that you want the kids to be aware of as an opportunity, but not have them be weighed down by the pressure of having to win. I've changed my basic approach to pre-game motivation. I subscribe to the John Wooden theory that winning is what I need to worry about, and playing to their potential is what the players need to worry about. Winning will be a by-product of them reaching their potential. My message is, "Go out, play hard, play fast and have fun. Don't worry about the final score." If they worry about having to win; if this is the biggest game of their life or the biggest play of their life, does that create a sense of urgency or a sense of tension that defeats enhancing performance?

We play better when we are relaxed. When performing fine and gross motor movements, if players are tense and on edge or go past the optimum arousal level, they won't play up to their full potential.

For myself in golf, when I try and swing the hardest, or try to kill the ball, often, bad things will result. When I am relaxed and I believe this shot is going to be an easy shot, it will go farther and better. It is a relaxation of muscles and allowing muscle memory to take over- "neuro-muscular patterning."

The confidence factor is not brash and cocky; it is an internalized belief. At the end of the game, if the game is close, the team believes they are going to find a way to win. We believe that we will win; because we have been there before, because we don't have the peaks and valleys of emotional arousal that occur.

Maybe we succeed because of their understanding what I am asking of them which is- "Play hard, play fast, and have fun. And the game is never over till it's over." It means that we are never out of a game, no matter what the score is. Our players have done a nice job of understanding what playing to their potential means.

Which do you prefer- the favorite or underdog role?

It's harder to handle the favorite role than the underdog role. As an underdog, you can use that as a motivational tool. When you are the favorite, you have to prepare your team to understand that the other team uses you as a goal, and they have something to prove by beating you. So we're going to get their A game, and as such, we have to prepare for that target growing on our back. We need to respond with our best game, because we are going to get our opponent's best game.

We learned a lot this year from having that favorite role. Just talking about being a defending champion is not enough. There's a lot to knowing the psychology of what your opponent is thinking. If you know yourself and you know your opponent, you have a chance to win. If you don't, you are probably going to lose.

How do you create rapport with your players?

Meeting with each player on a one-on-one basis, where his own particular viewpoint can be listened to by the head coach, is extremely important. During those meetings, they talk and I listen.

I have questions if need be, but I ask them what they want to talk about. Questions like, "How's your family? Are you meeting your goals? What do you think about the people that coach you? Who are our leaders? Whom do you trust? Who's the toughest player on the team?" I want to know what they think, and I want them to tell me. Only 10%

of the kids will say something. If they say, "No, coach, there's nothing I have to talk about" then I say, "Tell me about who you are living with; how is your roommate situation? How's your family, academics, athletics, etc?"

It usually takes me about two weeks to talk with them all. I only meet with every kid about 15 minutes. With 110 players, it takes a while. If we don't get it done in 15 minutes, they have an opportunity to sign up for more time. I want them to know that I know more about them than just their name and their number. I know where they came from and what they want to accomplish. Then, I think that enhances that trust factor, that belief factor.

Players want unconditional love from the coach. They would like to know that we hold them of value. Whether we win or lose, whether they make the big play that won, or the play that lost the game for us, they need to know we still care about them. High school coaches do a great job of that.

At the college level, kids say, "I know you have to win; I know this is a business." Yes, but if I tell them to go out, have fun, play fast, and play hard and we play our best, I'm okay with that. The only time that I have a problem is if we don't play up to our potential, or we don't play as well as I think we are capable of in a game. Then the first person I look at is myself and then my coaches.

Describe a quality practice session.

Some players want to be yelled at- they don't feel like they are getting any attention unless they are being yelled at. But if a coach is spending too much time yelling, I say, "Time out; you're not doing as good a job of coaching or teaching as you need to; if you were, you wouldn't need to yell as much on the field." There is a certain amount of yelling that is indigenous to the situation; sometimes players will think you're not fired up if you don't yell. I'm okay with that too.

Bottom line- I'm looking for performance on the practice field. There's an old adage, "Practice doesn't make perfect. Perfect practice makes you perfect."

My favorite adage is, "Don't get by; get better." We know we can all put in a minimum amount of energy and just get by. Nobody will yell at me, and I'll just be one of the guys. I can also energize myself and help energize the people around me by putting a little bit more into it, and the results might be great and I'll get a chance to do something good and impact people around me." We talk about that a lot.

It's really important for players to set a standard of how hard they will work. When the players go against a hard working guy in practice, they know they have to go 100% against him, because he is always going to go 100%. If they go with a buddy system of "you go easy on me and I'll go easy on you, and we'll just get by;" that really bothers me. They don't get better. When these guys set their own standards for excellence and work 100%, then we're going to be a great team. Not with my yelling at them, or the other coaches yelling at them. When the players accept that role and that sense of maturity, not by trying to get out of things, but by doing things right, then we've arrived and have a chance for success.

What kind of team building activities have you done?

We have unity meetings, which are group meetings where you discuss questions with six to seven players. We try to assemble the most diverse groups we can. We try and take a black kid from LA, a white kid from Eastern Oregon, a Hispanic kid, a Samoan, etc. to create a diverse group. Every time we meet, you have a different group, so you are meeting new people.

The questions go from generic questions with simple answers to questions about race and socioeconomic status, or religious beliefs. The meetings last about an hour and a half. Coaches are included. We do it with the incoming freshmen, and the total team in the fall and the spring. The last one in spring usually doesn't have the coaches involved.

We will also use various interactive games to create opportunities to study problem-solving. We also have a mentor program, where we put the younger players with a more experienced player at their position.

We also have a cross referencing thing for fall camp roommates. We will put the remaining upper classmen as roommates who ordinarily wouldn't know or workout with each other, such as receivers with defensive linemen, db's with o-linemen, etc. We're trying to get them to know each other as friends, rather than just teammates. It's for creating commonalty and breaking down the barriers. We are trying to create stronger family bonds and trust.

What is your team's routine before each game?

Friday night I share motivational thoughts that I want them to take with them to the game. These include what has occurred in the past, what we would like to have happen and specific things I want them to be aware of for this game. I want them to consider an overriding principle of a life skill that they are learning, whether it's how to compete, how to handle adversity, how to get the best from yourself or how to defeat an opponent.

There are various tactics that I use. I bring up the idea of wanting to be the guy who makes the play; of accepting that role in a positive manner. I want them to have scripts such as, "I want the other players to run behind me; I want to make the tackle that saves the game; I want to make the catch." The knowledge that you have done those things before and remembering the feeling builds confidence.

"Think about the greatest catch you've ever made and that great feeling; how exciting and fun it is to feel your teammates pat you on the back. Visualize the crowd, hear the crowd, and remember how great that feels." I don't do that every game, but I talk about some aspect of visualizing these things.

One of the things I try to guard against is burning up too much nervous energy on Saturday (game) morning. Two to three hours before the game, we do things with a somewhat relaxed tempo. We do mental work, although with the defense, we stand up and clap in unison, and though it is a mental session, there is a physical component that requires participation. It's a unification of purpose.

Before the game, I go over very basic, standard communications. I shake everybody's hand. I delineate keys to victory. They involve physical, quantifiable things. There may be 8-10 points that I say every game.

Then we take a moment of silence; all of us are linked together, holding hands, taking a knee. I usually talk for another minute about psychological and motivational aspects of the game. It might be detailing that we want to play hard or we want to play fast or we want to finish the plays, or that we want to play one inch out of control.

Sometimes I have more of a passion for a particular game; sometimes the game itself takes on a life of its own. Every game there is a need to create the desire to play well and give your best effort. Anything less is cheating yourself and your teammates.

For an every-down player, any play on any down can be a game-changing play. If you can't do it, get someone else in there. We're a team, so it's trying to instill a confidence both individually and as a team.

We're prepared, we have a great plan; we've been here before, etc. If it's a home game, I tell them to think about Autzen Stadium, and how the fans love us. The fans feed off of us. and we feed off the fans. We want the mindset that we can't lose, but that it still takes effort. Respect all, fear none.

I continually talk about everything being a battle. We should expect the best from our opponent, and we must be prepared to handle that.

A lot of the visualization stuff is done for the individual, and not so much for the team. When I talk about the confidence factor, I don't talk as much about the individual as the team. The player is thinking, "If I work hard, I make everybody better: the guys next to me and behind me, not just myself."

When we go into a game, there's a trust factor that each person is going to do his job and that no one will have to do more than his share.

I don't say, "This is the most important game of our lives." I used to, but don't anymore. What if you lose that one? Then what? I try to make it as the one more step, and the next opportunity. We don't get a lot of opportunities. We only have 11 opportunities a year to earn a twelfth.

What do you say or do after losses?

1) You have to find a way to profit from a loss. What's gone is gone; you can't change it. It's in the books. As a coach you want the player to say, "I need to learn from it; I need to profit from it somehow. If I did play well, what did I do, and how did it happen? If I didn't play well, why didn't I? Can I quantify it, physically or mentally? Here's what I need to do next time."

The individual player tries to find ways to identify the problem and create a working plan to eradicate that problem, whether it's a physical problem, a mental one, or a pressure thing where he got too upset, excited or scared.

I have the players verbalize to me what the problem was which is hard for them to do. If it's negative, they don't want to talk about it; we both understand and determine what to do so poor performances won't happen again. I make them understand I'm not attacking them; that we just need to find out what happened. That way we have a better chance to get something done.

2) In film evaluation, there are two views of every play, a sideline view and an end zone view. There is very little gray area left in football. We pretty much know where a guy lines up and if he did his technique right or wrong. There is no hiding; there are no excuses. The sooner the player learns that, the sooner he understands the accountability factor. That allows him to get better and gets past that idea of "it's somebody else's fault, or it's something that I couldn't control." We try to keep things under the young man's control.

Describe some motivational or disciplinary approaches you have used with athletes that weren't successful.

I think we have all had athletes that for some reason just don't respond. I've tried doing it in an individual manner. I have a policy of three strikes, and you're out- probation, suspension, then dismissal.

I've tried to invoke peer pressure. Sometimes that works, sometimes it doesn't. I ask other players who know him to help him. For example, if he has a problem going to class, they try to help him get to class. I tell them, "As a teammate, as part of our 'family,' we need to help each other, and he needs your help."

Anytime you can use a reward system versus a punishment system, you are better off. The other thing I learned is that the kids really want to play. The worst thing you can do with them is to not let them play. As coaches, the one thing we control is playing time. Getting on the field is what every young man wants to do. So knowing that they could lose playing times holds them somewhat accountable to the rules.

I tell them, "We're family and as such, I am the titular head of the family. Sometimes I will make decisions you won't like. My decisions are aimed at trying to please the majority and things that I can live with. These are things we have to do to keep the program moving forward. If you can't do it, then you must not want to be part of it."

How did you help make your players believe they could be successful?

When I got here in 1989, there wasn't a tremendous football tradition. In fact, the tradition was one you wouldn't want to talk about at all. One of the ways we countered that was talking about creating tradition, our own tradition.

Challenging the players to think of themselves in a more positive manner than others thought of themselves, and to act in that manner was pivotal. And then choosing to believe that success would occur.

Can you give a specific example?

Before the win over Texas in the Holiday Bowl game, I used a line from U.S. Navy officer William Driscoll, an instructor for top combat fighter pilots. He talked about wanting the pilots to fly 'one inch out of control- right on the edge.' And it just struck home to me, because we weren't going to beat Texas, in my opinion, by being well-centered and well-grounded and basically fundamental. We needed to be on the edge. We needed to be in their face, and in their mind. We needed to play almost out of control, like when you've done something athletic and you regain your balance and say, "Wow, what did I just do?"

That was my pregame talk, and I owe it all to him (Driscoll.) The key thing is not to play tight. We didn't talk about winning. We talked about playing to our potential, and the best way to play to your potential is to be relaxed, and the best way to be relaxed is to have fun and play on the edge.

What are your thoughts on team rules?

If someone breaks a rule and it's relatively minor, the assistant coach who works with him will handle it. Sometimes the assistant coach and I both meet with the player. You can't have 10 or 11 people dispensing discipline. So we standardize the disciplinary process, adhere to the code and I am the ultimate arbitrator for all situations. We say, "The Duck stops here," in my office.

Interview by Kay Porter, PhD., Author of "The Mental Athlete":
www.thementalathlete.com

- PART 2 -

THE
SPORTS
PSYCHOLOGY
INTERVIEWS

- 22 -

DR. GREG DALE: COACHES GUIDE TO SUCCESSFUL PRESEASON TEAM BUILDING

Duke University Sport Psychologist Greg Dale is the author of "101 Team Building Activities" and "It's a Mental Thing!: 5 Keys to Improving Performance and Enjoying Sport."

Obviously group dynamics are going to vary with the loss of some veterans and the addition of some younger players each new season. What do you recommend for pre-season icebreakers in order for the players to get to know each other better?

First, you want to reinforce the importance of passing down a positive culture from one generation to the next. It's important to talk to the upperclassmen about this.

Second, anything you can do to create an opportunity for a newer players t divulge information about him/herself and reveal things about him/herself such as talking about someone who has made a difference in his/her life and helped him/her get to the current situation. Or a player could talk about the proudest or most embarrassing moment s/he has had in his/her life.

Just simple things like that where they can draw certain pictures of those moments. It is really funny how people laugh and have a good time with that icebreaker as well.

I think it is important to establish a big brother/ little brother or big sister/little sister program where you make a connection with those young ones coming in. New players should try to connect with one particular athlete at the upper level. The older player will take on a mentoring role.

Can you briefly describe a few "battle tested" activities that would work well as part of a pre-season team building activity?

Anytime you can get your team away and take them on a retreat of some kind is ideal. Adventure-based activities are very helpful. For example, last year the Duke lacrosse team went whitewater rafting. It was really good because it was something that lots of these kids had never faced before. They were definitely outside their comfort zones. A couple of the rafts actually capsized, and they had to work really well together as a team to get back into the raft.

It was interesting to see how the team referred back to that experience during the year to talk about how they got through it and how it really brought them together. They said if they could get through that, they can get through anything they have to do during the season. So these kinds of adventure things are really helpful in bonding a team together.

Our Duke women's soccer team is going into the mountains, and they will do some physical training and set goals for the upcoming season.

On the fun side, they will do a skit night. They have to pick a theme and perform some skits. The team will certainly have a good time with that.

What about high school teams who might not have the resources to go on a trip?

The kids could get together and have a sleepover at the gym. (It's a good idea to get parents to volunteer as monitors.) They could do the skit night things as well. The goal is to begin to establish the culture and the environment that you want on that team.

Role-playing where the team starts talking about the different situations that could be challenging for us this year is a great exercise.

The players could discuss what they would do if the team is down at halftime or that officials are making really bad calls. Or it could be that people aren't doing the right thing off of the field.

You want to discuss various scenarios, and then have the team role-play ineffective or poor ways to deal with those. They will have a good laugh with that. Then have them role-play more effective ways or more mentally tough ways to respond to those same situations. Doing this helps set the tone from the beginning of the year that, "This is how we are going to react when things are not going our way."

Role-playing like this really gets the message across that there are better way to handle adverse things.

For coaches or sport psychologists who are leading team-building activities, what are the most important factors to keep in mind from an organizational standpoint? For example, how does one determine which activities will work best with a certain team? How does one evaluate a team culture?

From an organizational standpoint, keep activities simple, fun and challenging. They need to be simple enough so they can be fairly easily set up and explained.

But the exercises should also be challenging, and they should also have a message that relates to what we are doing on our team or our sport. It is one thing to do those activities that are fun but quite another to show how the exercise relates to what you are trying to achieve as a group. In my 101 Team Building Activities book, there are questions provided at the end of each exercise that you can ask to really bring it back to the sport. That's very important.

Early on with a new team, there is some trial and error. There are things I have done before that have just flopped. I thought they were the best things going, but for that particular team, it just didn't work. You could have done that same activity with another team, and it would have been awesome.

It's important to do your homework, especially early on. I recommend talking to the team leaders or captains. Whether you are a sports psychologist or a coach, ask them, "I am thinking about doing such and such activity, what do you think?"

Most of the time they will be very good about providing valuable information. They will say, "No, I don't think that will work" or "Yeah, that's a great idea."

But even then, there may be times when the team leaders thought an activity was good, but the team might not respond. So, again, there is lots of trial and error.

What are some common mistakes that coaches might make when putting together a team building activity?

The one thing I find when coaches do this is that they need to be careful about placing their own agenda on the thing from the very beginning.

They need to provide the framework and then back away. They can say, "Here is an activity, here is what we are going to do, and let's see what comes out of it."

Don't say, "Guys, we really need to work on our communication so this is what we are going to do." Or "I think you guys really need to work on your trust- you don't trust each other, so this is what we are going to do."

The coach is putting his or her emphasis on the exercise right away. I recommend giving them an activity, telling them what you want them to do, and then allow them to talk about what they got out of it without you putting your emphasis on it from the very beginning.

Developing a team motto can be a powerful rallying cry to refer back to at different points during the season. How can a team effectively develop such a motto during the pre-season period?

You have to get them to think about it from the very beginning. There is an exercise I call "Team Symbol" that works well.

After a couple weeks of practice, before you really get into your pre-season games or scrimmages, you need to get each kid to bring in 2 symbols. One symbol represents what their role is on the team or what he or she brings to the team. Some people bring in a megaphone because they are the vocal person on the team. Some will bring in a bottle of glue because that teammate feels she is the glue that holds the team together. A guy might bring in a nail because he feels that he is tough as nails.

The second symbol is what players think symbolizes this team. Players can be very creative in what they bring.

For example, one athlete brought in a miniature house. She talked about how she felt like she was this part of the house. The team latched onto that concept and their motto was "building the house." Everybody had different roles in building that house. Some people had really small roles, and others had bigger roles.

Each player must present his or her symbols in front of the group. They have to stand up and say this is my symbol, and this is what I think our team symbol is. Then the team votes on the one that they think is the best symbol for their team and develop a motto around that.

An important question to ask the group is, "What are the main themes we need to focus on as a team?" They should be able to find one to rally around.

Are there any particular exercises that seem to work better with men vs. women teams?

A lot of this comes down to how you present it to the athletes. If you are enthusiastic about it and tell them that they are going to laugh at themselves a little bit, most of the time the exercises are well received.

I will say that typically girls in my experience seem a little bit more comfortable with those activities where they have to reveal a lot about themselves. One big difference with guys is that they are little less likely to talk about the things that they struggle with- like their most embarrassing moment or whatever. Typically, our (male) egos are a little too big for that.

I got a great idea from (former Duke basketball player Jay Williams) and started using it with some of the teams I work with, tug-of-war contests. I didn't know how our women would respond, but the Lacrosse team had a great time with that.

I have also done a banana relay where guys have to sit on the floor- all of them facing the same direction and pass a banana with their feet from one end to the other and back again. I just did that with the top 100 high school boys soccer players in the country. They had a great time, but I wasn't sure how that exercise would go over.

How can you relate the exercise back to what they will face on the team?

Let's use the tug-of-war example. You divide your team and put 11 on one side and 11 on the other. You can do starters vs. non-starters or whatever.

Have them do the tug-of-war, and see who wins that. Then the next time you can say that one team needs to encourage each other and communicate really well together. But this group over here, you are not allowed to say anything at all. They will see the difference and 9 times out of 10, the team that is encouraging each other and communicating is going to win.

Another variation is to have one person on the rope who is not allowed to pull at all. What happens is that team will lose very quickly. This demonstrates a great point that, "Hey, you may be out there on the field but if you all aren't busting your tail or not doing your part, then look what happens. Everybody on this team has got to be pulling their weight all the time in order for us to be successful."

As a coach, you can talk a lot about each individual's importance, but when they experience something like that first hand, the concept is right there for them. That is how you relate it back to their sport.

We have to realize that people learn things in different ways. Some people you can just tell them, and they will learn it.

Most people, if they can experience something, are going to learn it and remember it a whole lot better. If you can be creative in the way that you present these activities and relate it back to the sport, players are going to be more likely to remember that.

Let's say a coach is all fired up about a particular team building activity, yet the players put up some resistance or don't seem too interested. Is there anything you can recommend to capture their attention and help them grasp the bigger picture of why the team is doing a team-building activity?

As a coach, you can reinforce the idea that things aren't always going to go your way. You, as the disgruntled player, are not going to like everything we do. We, as coaches, are convinced that this is the best thing for the team.

The athlete might not like the role they have on the team, or doing conditioning when it is 90 degrees outside, but players have to work on changing their attitude. You need to begin to establish the mindset that how they approach the situation is what counts.

Maybe the player doesn't think this is a fun activity or that it's not going to be relevant. There should be nobody on the team that would be able to tell that the player has those feelings by the way they act or the things they say.

Even if they aren't sold on the merit of a particular activity, they can act like it is important to them. When they do this, they won't affect teammates in a negative way.

Here is what you may say to those who are putting up resistance, "As the leader of this team, I need you all to buy into this even if you don't feel like it. You have to act like you like it; even if you have to fake it until you make it."

Relate the team-building exercise to other experiences that they are going to go through during the season. When things aren't going their way or it is not exactly the way they want it, ask the question, "How are we going to respond to the situation?" These exercises will help our team respond the way we must to be successful.

- 23 -

DR. KEN RAVIZZA: ROUTINES TO MAXIMIZE ATHLETIC PERFORMANCE

Ken Ravizza is one of the pioneers in the field of sport psychology. He is the author of "Heads Up Baseball". His consulting work spans Olympic, NFL, and Major League Baseball teams. As the sport psychologist for Cal State Fullerton, he has worked with national champion teams in baseball, softball and gymnastics.

Why are routines important?

Routines are important because they give athletes something that they have control over. Focusing on what they can control will help them in their consistency of performance. There are certain things they can do to get themselves where they need to be each time they compete.

What do routines do mentally for the athlete?

They allow them to have something specific to focus on. For example, let's say you are performing at 7:00 p.m. When does the performance begin? It begins long before 7:00. What the athlete does leading up that performance has a great impact. There are many things in the time period leading up to the contest that athletes can do to get themselves mentally ready.

Can you give a specific example for routines during and before a performance using an ice hockey goalie?

This player's routine begins back when he leaves the hotel or his home to go to the rink. He's checking and double-checking his bag to make sure he has everything. He may do some visualization at this time for what he wants to accomplish later that night.

Once he arrives at the venue where he'll be performing, he walks in. Let's say he hasn't performed there before. He will take some time to briefly familiarize himself with that facility. He then would select a focal point. That's a key concept here. It's part of the funneling process. This goalie has got a broad focus before the game. Now as the minutes get closer to game time and he gets ready to perform, he needs to narrow that focus down.

A focal point will remind him of the work that he has done in training and that he is prepared for this event. It reminds him to trust himself and his performance.

What's an example of a focal point?

Maybe it's the flag he sees when he walks in. It could be a championship banner or even an advertising sign. It could be the "section seven" sign because he likes the number 7. The idea here is that the focal point serves as a reminder that the goalie has paid his dues, and he is ready to compete.

It also serves as a method to get his energy outwardly focused. That's where a goalie has got to be. He's got be out on the puck; he can't be inside his head. If he's internal, he's not going to be as quick; he's not going to see things as clearly. That focal point is something that helps him get comfortable with the environment. It establishes a particular point that he can focus in on.

Olympic athletes have said how helpful it was when they've gone to the Olympic games and they look around that giant stadium to pick a focal point. It is a way to ground them and get them back where they need to be mentally. (This same technique can be used by any athlete, regardless of the sport, Ed).

Back to the hockey example. After checking out the rink, he goes into the locker room to change from his street clothes to the hockey gear. The changing of the clothes is a key time period. Try to keep it similar each game. Then he's going to go through getting any treatment or stretching and doing those types of things. Then he goes out to the ice. He's going to skate a little bit to get the blood flowing. Then he's going to go down around the net and do his housekeeping. By that I mean that he is going to familiarize himself with the ice and with the net. He needs to get comfortable with it because no two goals are the same. Next, he looks up at the focal point and that is his cue to get ready to go- the game is about to start.

Do you think that from the time in the locker room to the time you get on the ice, everything should be close to the same each night?

Yes, the same routine for that individual. But each guy is different. Some guys are more compulsive about it. Other guys are a little more laid back about it, but they need to be consistent. Some guys are going to have walkman's going (or other musical devices), other guys are going to play cards, some will like to joke around, other guys are going to have their chair facing into their locker, deep in concentration. What becomes important is that each players needs to do what works best for him.

How does a player figure that out?

He looks at the times when he performed well- what did he do on those nights? Then he looks at the times when he performed poorly, what did he do then and how did he go about his business? Obviously, the player should find patterns of success or failure and stick to what has worked for that individual.

Describe the differences between a ritual and a routine.

Athletes need to differentiate between peak performance routines and rituals or superstitions. Ritual means that the power is in a force outside of yourself- it's attributed to the lucky underwear, the lucky jock, whatever. Routines are things that I, as an athlete, have total control over.

I'm not saying that rituals and superstitions are bad- some athletes like doing them, and they probably aren't going to change. But with routines, athletes need to be systematic in the way they go about it. Part of the routine is that you've got to get comfortable with yourself in the environment in which you will perform. Then you've got to get comfortable with the state of your body on that particular day. This part of the routine can involve athletic trainers work, a massage, or stretching.

Then a player has to get comfortable with himself and his skills. He needs to practice working on basic techniques. Finally, he starts zoning in to getting himself ready to perform. The funnel starts out broad and gets more narrow as the competition time gets closer. First, the venue, then self, then technique, and finally playing the sport. The athlete moves from a wide spectrum to a very narrow spectrum.

For the hockey goalie, he needs to get to the point where he is totally locked in. But when the puck is down at the far end, he may stand up, come out of his area a little bit, and then they go back into the net area. When he goes back into the net area to defend the goal, he needs to lock in mentally.

What happens when a goal is scored or a bad play occurs?

After a goal is scored, then he has to have a routine that includes some way of releasing the goal. He's ticked off; he's upset. He needs to release it- whether it's pounding the side of the cage or whether it's adjusting the mask or whatever else it may be. But then he needs to regroup and get back into it. So he has to have a set routine to let go and get himself back into the game where he needs to be.

- 24 -

DR. ALAN GOLDBERG: PSYCHOLOGICAL TECHNIQUES THAT HELPED UCONN WIN TWO NCAA CHAMPIONSHIPS

Slumpbusting expert Dr. Alan Goldberg has worked extensively with the University of Connecticut as a consulting sport psychologist, including their national champion Men's Soccer and Basketball teams.

How did you help the soccer team come up with goals and a mission statement?

The run at the national championship started the evening after they lost the semi-final game the previous year. We met after that game and again in the spring and planned for the next season, set goals, and drew up a mission statement and list of commitments.

I facilitated the process- they came up with mission. The coaches weren't involved. Once completed, the goals were very similar to that of the coaches.

We talked about what it would take to win the national championship. I asked them what qualities a national championship team would have. Then we set some standards that they wanted everyone to follow. If the team is committed to the mission because they have put it together, the coach is going to get a lot more out of them rather than the coaches coming up with the mission and telling the team, "now go do it."

It was National Championship or bust for the team. How did you help them deal with that kind of pressure?

I told them to be completely oblivious to it. In team meetings, we talked about working towards goals on a daily basis.

For example, at the end of practice one day, the players were doing sprints around the field. Some of the guys were getting too winded to continue. Coach Reid had them come over and started to talk about what it felt like last year in Charlotte when they lost the 3 overtime game.

The point is, you talk about and think about goals every day to help you go harder. The time to forget about goals is when you are competing. Despite the fact they had a mission in the future (NCAA title), I kept them focused on the present and staying in the now.

How do you bring kids back into the present when they beat themselves up mentally?

The key is having awareness. The athletes have to know when they are drifting and losing focus. Having awareness is the foundation of control. I helped them become aware of where they needed to put their focus. I also asked them what "triggered" them to lose focus, i.e. helping them figure out what was going on in their minds to trap them and take them to the wrong place mentally. Losing focus and not coming back is where the real damage is caused.

I would ask questions like, "Why are they losing focus?" Or, "What are you doing at this moment that is getting you into trouble?"

The key is building in an early warning system. This allows the player to take action before the bombs start to drop. When it gets to that point, you really lose control. Once it reaches crisis mode, it's too late to do anything.

We talk a lot about uncontrollables or UC's. In any given game, there are tons of things out of the athlete's control. When the athlete starts to focus on UC's, their stress level goes up, confidence goes down, and performance suffers.

Examples of UC's are the physical play of another team, poor calls, field conditions, or how much playing time an athlete is getting.

I didn't want them on the bench stewing about not getting playing time, because when they did go in, they wouldn't be ready.

Did you do any specific team building exercises?

One exercise is called the winner's circle. The guys would break into three groups of 8 and each person would say something they like or respect about the teammate standing next to them in the circle.

We asked them to define what it would like to be a winner. The answer we all came up with is that winners took risk and did the impossible. They put themselves on the line.

Speaking in front of a group is very hard for many people. Even more difficult is speaking to a group of your peers, especially when the subject is your feelings about that group. Before the national semi-finals, I had some of the players stand up and talk about what it meant to be playing on this team. It was a very powerful motivator. Everyone was encouraged, but no one was forced to speak.

Were there any other key factors to the team's success?

One of the things that is crucial for any team who wants to go all the way is acceptance of role players. The soccer team had 27 players, 7 or 8 of who of them did not dress out for games.

You don't win a championship with just the starters or main back-ups. For Uconn, every day in practice the role players drove the starters, and pushed them to get better. They were lauded for their efforts, and we kept that going all season long. They have the toughest job on the team, as any support player does. They must be made to feel like they are an important part of the team. So many players have a "what's in it for me attitude?" They must be made to feel like they are contributing to the team mission.

You have to have an arrangement in place before the season that "these are the rules" and when you break them, you are deliberately hurting your teammates. The message is, "Hey, you are making a conscious choice to screw over your teammates. You aren't really getting away with something; you are affecting everyone by making a poor decision."

How can you get athletes to stretch themselves, especially after a losing season when they are afraid to commit to goals?

I would simply tell that team, "It's unacceptable. Previous failure is no excuse not to set goals." Being afraid of not achieving them is never a good reason not to set goals. Athletes have to know that if they never fail, they will never be successful. The purpose of the goal setting process isn't just to reach goals; it's to push them to higher levels of performance.

One of themes in our Uconn meetings was "get comfortable with being uncomfortable." We talked a lot about getting outside of their comfort zone in various ways. Examples include working on weak points, playing tougher opponents, and pushing themselves physically. You can't play afraid or worried about making mistakes, which only leads to disaster.

Describe your relationship with Coach Reid and the team.

He was very open to the process. I had full access to the team. Anyone who wanted to see me individually could come anytime they wanted. This past season I had 8 or 9 meetings with the team, none of which involved the coaching staff.

The coaches would refer people to me regarding specific issues. Some examples are a kid who makes a mistake and hangs on to it, a kid who beats himself up to the point where it gets in the way of his performance, or a kid who has trouble controlling his emotions and puts the team at risk.

Some players would come to see me because they had their own issues to talk about. That's the secret here. It's a question of getting to know them and establishing trust. I worked with some of them since they were freshman. I made it clear to them from the start, "Hey, I work for you guys."

The second part of the interview concerned Dr. Goldberg's work with the Men's Basketball team.

What were the major concerns of the players you worked with?

Handling pressure, dealing with mistakes and setbacks, and being able to bounce back quickly. When they make a mistake, they wanted to learn to be able to maintain their focus so they wouldn't get caught up and worried about getting pulled out of the game.

Outside pressure was a big issue. Friends, family and media saying, "You know you should be scoring more or playing more, etc." I taught skills that helped them keep focused on the things that are important for them to do their best. I emphasized letting the game come to them instead of trying to make something happen.

A lot of the UConn players were under a microscope most of the year. They were covered by something like 18 papers nationally. We talked about not reading the papers and magazines because that stuff gets you into trouble. You start reading the press, and it gets in your head. The players I talked to were aware of what happens when they did read too much of their own press. So they were smart enough to understand not to pay a lot of attention to that stuff.

The media talked about Coach Calhoun and never getting his team to the Final Four. There was an implication that he wasn't that good of a coach. Otherwise, he would have gotten his team there. The players didn't get caught up in that.

Where was the team mentally during the NCAA tournament, in partic- ular, in the championship game?

As the tournament progressed, they played better and better. They did what they needed to do, and I think mentally they were where they needed to be. When they went out on the court against Duke in the championship game, they were not intimidated. They believed and felt they could win.

Being in the right frame of mind is a question of focusing on the right stuff. They didn't care about Duke's reputation, or that everybody had been saying that this was Duke's tournament.

What specific issues did you help players overcome?

One issue for players is wanting to play well and wanting to do their best. I told them if they get too caught up in wanting to play well, they won't. The question is getting them to focus on and think about the things that they can control.

I talked a lot about staying away from uncontrollables. Those are the things that cause pressure and tie you up in knots. You can't really play in control wanting to play well. What you can control is keeping your head in the game and doing the things that you normally do. If you do that, playing well will take care of itself. I tried to get them to understand that the game is inside of you, and you just want to relax and let it come out.

Another issue was bouncing back from mistakes. If you do something and get pulled out of the game, learning not to hang on to the mistake the next time you get in.

I tried to teach athletes how to stay in the now. You make a mistake, it is gone, it is an uncontrollable, and you can't get it back. You don't want to be thinking about the mistake, or thinking about the coaches, or thinking, "What if I get yanked again?"

Athletes need to be focused on what is going on right in the moment. Getting athletes in the right mindset, to relax, to trust themselves and to focus on the right things. I tried to make the player switch his focus away from other people's expectations, including the crowd, the fans and the families.

Can you describe a specific technique you used to help a player?

With a number of players, it is getting them to go back and think about and re-live when they played their best. "What were the elements that happened when you played your best? How did it feel? What did you focus on? What were you thinking about?' I want them to understand that good performance is always inside of them when they repeat those same elements.

What was a primary cause of poor performance?

They are pressing themselves, thinking too much, trying too hard, and concentrating on the wrong things.

I explained that when they were playing well they weren't thinking about mistakes, thinking about getting benched, or thinking about expectations from parents.

For two or three players, I had to get them back in touch with the idea that having fun is the ticket to playing well. They were under the misconception, "If I score 12 or 15 points, then I will have fun." That is backwards. If you are having fun, and in touch with why you play the game, then you are going to play well. Playing well is always a result of having fun because you are relaxed. The secret to doing well in any sport is being relaxed and if you are having fun, that helps you do that. Then you get into being creative on the court and making things happen.

- 25 -

DR. JIM TAYLOR: ADDRESS THE 4 MOST CRITICAL AREAS TO PREVENT SLUMPS

Dr. Taylor is a former sport psychology consultant to the USTA and USA Triathlon. He has authored 600 articles and 12 books including the best seller "Positive Pushing: How to Raise a Successful and Happy Child".

What are the primary causes for a performance slump?

The causes of performance slumps can be grouped into four general categories. First, perhaps the most common cause of slumps, is a physical problem. These difficulties include fatigue, minor injuries, and lingering illness.

Second, slumps may be due to subtle changes in technique that occur during the course of a season. These changes may be in the execution of the skill or in the timing of the movement.

Third, slumps may begin with changes in an athlete's equipment, e.g., loosening of string tension on a tennis racquet or a different weight of a new baseball bat. Particularly in those sports that require elaborate equipment, there is a precise balance between equipment and technique. As a result, a slight change in equipment may alter technique, thereby hurting performance.

Fourth, slumps can be caused by psychological factors. Furthermore, the mental contributors may be related to or independent of the athletic involvement. For example, a particularly poor performance may reduce confidence and increase anxiety, which could lead to a prolonged drop in performance. In contract, issues away from competition such as family difficulties, financial problems, and school struggles may distract concentration, increase stress, and decrease motivation, thus resulting in a performance decline.

How can slumps best be addressed?

The best way to deal with slumps is to prevent them from happening. Slumps can best be prevented by carefully examining the four primary areas that cause them.

1) Physical. As discussed above, many slumps begin with physical difficulties. More specifically, slumps are often caused by the normal physical wear and tear of the competitive season. As a result, perform-ance slumps may be prevented by paying attention to various factors that influence an athlete's physical state.

One important area that can be addressed is physical condition. Quite simply, athletes who are well-conditioned will be less susceptible to fatigue, injury, and illness. Consequently, a rigorous off-season physi-cal training program and a competitive season physical maintenance program will help minimize slumps due to physical breakdown.

Second, a significant part of slump prevention is rest. In other words, physical deterioration can be lessened by actively incorporating rest into athletes' training and competitive regimens. Adequate rest can be assured in several ways. Days off can be built into the weekly training schedule. For example, in sports with weekend competitions, having mandatory Mondays off is a good way to ensure that athletes are able to recover from the prior week's training and the stresses of the previ-ous days' competition.

Third, athletes can reduce the quantity and increase the quality of train-ing as the season progresses. This approach will allow athletes to maintain a high level of health and energy right through the end of the season. This is especially important in sports that have lengthy seasons such as baseball, tennis, and golf.

Fourth, planning a responsible competition schedule can also prevent slumps. Perhaps the most demanding aspect of sports involvement is the actual competition. Competing in too many events is both physi-cally and mentally draining and may be counterproductive for the ath-lete. As a result, athletes and coaches need to select the competitions that are most important for the athletes and to avoid scheduling events that serve no specified purpose in the athlete's seasonal competitive plan.

Fifth, scheduling time off about three weeks before an important competition, particularly when it is towards the end of the season, can help to ensure a high level of performance. This strategy allows athletes to recover from previous competitions, overcome nagging injuries and illness, focus attention on the upcoming competition, and prepare for the final push toward that competition. Most fundamentally, the best way to reduce the likelihood of a slump due to physical causes is for athletes to listen to their bodies. They need to acknowledge fatigue, injury, and illness and when any are evident, they should be dealt with immediately. Simply put, athletes must learn to work hard and rest hard.

2) Technical or Form Related. Slumps that are caused by technical changes can also be prevented by taking steps to maintain sound technique, which results in strong performance. First, technique is best developed during the off-season when the primary focus is on technical improvement, and there is adequate time to fully acquire the skills. Minimizing technical work done during the competitive season can help prevent technically induced slumps. Working on technique may not only disturb the technique that is producing good performance, it may also hurt performance by reducing confidence and distracting concentration. In addition, maintaining a video library of good technique and performances can be used by athletes and coaches to remind them of proper technique and to compare current with past technique.

3) Equipment or Technological. The best way to prevent technologically or equipment related performance slumps is to maintain equipment at its highest performance level.

For example, tennis racquets should be restrung before their tension changes or if a favorite baseball bat is broken, it should be replaced by another one of identical weight and balance.

4) Psychological. Performance slumps that are caused by psychological factors can be addressed at two levels. First, for those difficulties that arise directly from competition, it is important to have athletes engaged in a regular mental training program. This approach will develop athletes' mental skills in areas such as self-confidence, anxiety, concentration, and motivation, thereby making them more resilient to the negative psychological effects of periodic poor performance. In addition, following poor performance, it is necessary for athletes to actively combat these negative psychological effects by employing these mental skills. This will prevent them from getting caught in a self-perpetuating vicious cycle of low self-confidence and poor performance.

Second, for those difficulties that occur away from the sport, it is necessary for athletes to work them out quickly and effectively. In addition, the previously learned mental skills can used to leave these difficulties off the field, so that, at least during competition, athletes are able to maintain their proper focus and intensity, thus preventing a drop in performance.

- 26 -

DR. ROB GILBERT: STORYTELLING TO MOTIVATE AND INSPIRE

Dr. Rob Gilbert is a motivational sports psychologist and author of four books including "Read This Book Tonight to Help You Win Tomorrow", "Good to Great Golf", and "Gilbert on Greatness".

Dr. Gilbert, please tell us how coaches can use stories to motivate and inspire athletic teams.

Knute Rockne of Notre Dame is still considered college football's all-time greatest coach. His first star player was running back George Gipp. Near the end of his senior season, Gipp became gravely ill. And with his coach at his bedside, George Gipp died on December 14, 1929.

Eight years later an uninspired Notre Dame team was about to play the undefeated Cadets of West Point. Just before they took the field, Rockne gathered his team around him in the locker room and told them about the final moments of George Gipp's life...

Gipp said, "Rock, this is it. Nothing can be done."

Rockne pleaded, "George, there must be *something* I can do for you."

Gipp finally said, "OK, Rock, I'll tell you what you can do for me. There's going to come a time when you're going to want to win a game more than anything else in the world. When that time comes, tell them to WIN ONE FOR THE GIPPER."

Rockne took a long look around the locker room. Then he said, "What about it boys?"

That day the emotion on the field was unbelievable. The final score:

173

Notre Dame 12   Army 6

What did Rockne do? Why did it work? And will it work for you?

Rockne followed the four principles of storytelling. If you do what Rockne did, you'll be able to get results like Rockne got.

Here are the four principles:
> #1) Tell the right story.
> #2) Tell it to the right group.
> #3) Tell it at the right time.
> #4) Tell it the right way.

Have you ever had a coach like Knute Rockne who always seemed to motivate you like no one else ever could? Have you ever had a history teacher who made the past come so alive that you felt as though you were actually there? Have you ever been totally mesmerized by a speaker?

Chances are that one of the reasons the coach, the teacher, and the speaker had such a powerful effect on you is that they used stories.

Here's a good example:

"It's late at night, and you can't wait to get home. Your car is literally flying down the highway. Your thoughts are interrupted by the flashing lights in your rearview mirror. You pull off to the side of the road. Eventually the state trooper walks to your car, looks down at you, and sternly requests your license and registration. As he waits you begin to say…"

Now, if you've ever been in that situation and you've talked your way out of a ticket, I don't know exactly WHAT you said, but I'll bet I know HOW you said it- you told the officer a story.

A story of why you had to get home so quickly because of a family emergency. Or a story about a personal crisis. Or even a story about why you couldn't afford to get another ticket.

Why did you tell the officer a story? Simple. Stories work. Why are stories so powerful? A story is about something that happened in the PAST, that is told in the PRESENT, and that will be remembered in the FUTURE.

As a university professor for 25 years, I've noticed that when I use stories, three things happen almost instantly; my students give me their total attention, they physically relax, and they let down their conscious resistance. As a result of these three things, something else happens-they remember the stories.

A good story told well sticks. When I see former students, some of them remind me of the stories I told them ten or fifteen years ago! So when you want to motivate, persuade, or inspire, stories will work much better than the straightforward presentation of facts and ideas.

Principle #1) TELL THE RIGHT STORY. Obviously your players have to relate to the story, but it doesn't have to be about sports.

Principle #2) TELL IT TO THE RIGHT GROUP. You can use your own judgment to tell if you have a team that will be really receptive to story-telling.

Principle #3) TELL IT AT THE RIGHT TIME. When you tell a story, it's like giving the listener a gift. Everyone likes to hear stories, and everyone likes to receive gifts. Part of the power of both stories and gifts is the timing of when they are delivered. To be effective they have to be delivered at the right time.

In telling a story to motivate, persuade, or inspire, you have to develop the intuitive sense of WHEN to tell that certain story. Part of Rockne's genius was that he waited eight years before he told his team to "win one for the Gipper."

Principle #4) TELL THE STORY IN THE RIGHT WAY. No problem! You have the solution right in your hands. Here are seven of the most closely guarded secrets of the world's greatest storytellers. Once you start practicing these simple but powerful techniques, you'll graduate from being just another person who tells stories to a person who is a great storyteller.

Here are the six secrets of the world's greatest storytellers:

Technique #1. LESS IS MORE. One thing that stories and jokes have in common is that the shorter they are, the more powerful they become. Humor expert Larry Wilde said it this way, "The size of the laugh you get is inversely proportional to the number of words used to reach the punch line. Thus, the fewer words used, the bigger the laughs." It's exactly the same with stories.

Fred Astaire once said something about his dance routines that could be applied to speech making, storytelling, and a lot of other things. He said, "Get it 'till it's perfect, then cut two minutes."

Technique #2. THE POWER OF THE DRAMATIC...PAUSE. For any story to be effective, you have to get and keep the listener's attention and build their anticipation. One of the best ways to do this is to master the art of the "dramatic pause."

Great communicators have always used this. You can hear one of them on the radio every day, news commentator Paul Harvey. He's mastered the art of the pause. Listen to him, tape his broadcasts and study what he does.

WARNING: Be careful. Pausing at the *wrong* time can be dangerous. It can totally change the meaning you want to convey. For example, read the following two sentences out loud:

"What's that in the road ahead?"

"What's that in the road... a head?" Notice how the pause changes everything.

Technique #3. DAN RATHER, PETER JENNINGS, AND TOM BROKAW MAY BE HAZARDOUS TO YOUR STORYTELLING HEALTH.

News broadcasters report the news- they are not part of the news.

To tell stories powerfully, you can't stand apart from your story. You have to be a part of the story. In other words, you can't be a commentator. You have to be a participant. When you tell an emotional, personal story, the listener usually becomes riveted. The more you're into your story, the more they'll be. You can't expect the listener to be enthusiastic about your story unless you are.

Look at the word enthusiasm. The last four letters IASM form an acronym that stands for "I AM SOLD MYSELF." If you're not sold for the value, power, or beauty of the story, don't expect anyone else to be.

Technique #4. LET YOUR CHARACTERS SPEAK FOR THEM-SELVES. Don't report the story, act the story. But when using emotion, you have to become emotional at the right time.

In other words, when a character in the story is talking, say what they were saying as if they were actually saying it. The rule here is when you have a story that has dialogue, use emotion in the dialogue- not in the narrative.

For example, here is the wrong way to state something: *He got really mad* and said, "*I'm leaving.*"

The right way would place the emphasis on "I'm Leaving." He got really mad and said, "I'm leaving."

In the second example, the emotion is correctly placed in the dialogue. The dialogue is where you use the emotion.

This technique works magic because you're acting the part of the character(s) in the story. When you're animated, the story becomes animated, and it will captivate the listener.

Technique #5. BE CONVERSATIONAL. USE THE K.I.S.S. PRIN-CIPLE. In other words, Keep It Small & Short. This means that you should use *small* words and *short* sentences.

Remember, big words and long sentences impede the progression (sorry, I mean "stop the flow") of your story. Use small words. Use short sentences.

Technique #6. TAILOR THE STORY TO FIT YOUR AUDIENCE. To insure that your listener is into your story, you can't just RELATE it, you have to make your story as RELEVANT as possible to that person.

An effortless way to do it is to tell musicians stories about musicians. Tell students stories about students. Obviously, stories that show athletes or teams overcoming great odds to success would be where you could draw some of your most powerful material as a coach.

What is an example of a quick exercise that helps build team unity using storytelling?

Here is a storytelling technique that NEVER fails from my teaching experience.

Are you familiar with the acronym "MEGO?" MEGO stands for My Eyes Glaze Over. When I'm teaching a class and several students are in that "MEGO" state, I know exactly what to do.

I have everyone stand up and get a partner. Then I give them a topic like "A time in my life I felt really successful." I have each student tell his or her partner a personal success story for no more than 60 seconds.

As a result of this storytelling exercise, my students instantly become more energized and seem happier! Most importantly, my students' attention goes from "MEGO" to my communication. Once again, they're focused on their instructor or in your case, the coach.

- 27 -

DR. TONI ZIMMERMAN: SIMPLE EXERCISES TO STRENGTHEN TEAM UNITY

Toni Zimmerman is a marriage and family studies professor at Colorado State University. She formerly was a sport psychology consultant to athletic teams using family therapy techniques to build team unity.

Team-building is a continual process and is different each year. What are some good ways to get team-building started in a positive direction?

At the beginning of your calendar year, have team members write down a list of things that has helped build team unity in their past experience. Then have employees list issues or things that have really gotten in the way of team unity.

On a chalkboard, have a manager draw a line down the middle and list the positives on one side and the negatives on the other.

Involve the team by asking them about their past experiences when team unity has been a problem or you felt frustrated by it and times you felt like things were going really great.

Let the employees define what team unity is for themselves. Create an operational definition of things that work and don't work.

An example of a negative might be that team unity was destroyed when there was gossip, separate coalitions or cliques on a team. It might have been a team where a few members were kept on the outside of the circle.

After the list is completed, start at the top and address the issues raised. Take gossip, for example. The leader should ask the team members

"How can we stop this from happening?" or "How can we keep certain cliques out of this team?"

One idea might be to establish a team policy about worker interaction. If a conflict occurs between two people, they should try to resolve it first between themselves. There may be a need to go to the coach. The coach can then decide if the situation is important enough to talk about openly to the entire team. Otherwise drop it and move on.

On the positive side, there could be a team policy to always encourage and point out the best in somebody instead of picking on their faults.

When team members have input in making up their own rules and team philosophy, based on what they have experienced, they are far more likely to carry through with them. When you involve the team in trying to build team unity, you make it a very overt process. Trying to follow a certain five-step team-building plan usually won't work because each group of individuals involved in the process is different. But if certain procedures have worked in the past, certainly stick with them.

When should the team review how things are going?

Have another major meeting in two months to see what has been working or has not been working. Point out what has gone right. For example someone might say, "Man, I really thought it worked great when we took time to review the high points of the presentation, even after we lost the bid. We pointed out who did well in a losing effort. That built up team unity."

Re-visit that original chart frequently. Ask, "How are we doing in our weak areas? Are we keeping them under control? Where do we need to improve?"

Can you describe one or two exercises that all teams can use to build up team unity?

Gather in a room in a circle, and have each person on the team tell one unique thing about his/herself that no one else would know. Do this exercise twice a month so you get to know sides of a person that you wouldn't otherwise.

This brings out the personal side of people- they aren't just worker X or Y, but there are other aspects of their personality they feel comfortable in sharing. These are great icebreakers at the beginning of the year and to do at meetings throughout the year.

Here is a variation on the same exercise. Find out all you can about the person sitting next to you and then you introduce that person to the team. This exercise is best done with new hires during one of their first meetings. It can be a really fun way to get to know one another.

What are some ways to handle "problem" employees that don't seem to fit in?

I compare the situation to family therapy. In families, there is a tendency to give everyone an assigned role- the hero, the mischievous one, the smart one, or the whiny one. It's important to keep away from putting people in really defined boxes. You don't want to reduce people to a cliché. Instead get to know the person as far more than a one-dimensional characterization.

If someone is on the outside of the "circle" and doesn't seem to blend in, get the team to brainstorm. The question should be asked, "If they aren't part of our family, how can we bring them in?" One idea is to give them another job or role. Ideas include asking them to mentor new employees, or getting them to assist the manager for an upcoming project. Come up with creative ways to help them blend in and assimilate. These are involvement devices that help that employee feel he or she is part of the team. The mistake that we make with people who don't fit in is to push them farther and farther outside the circle so they don't bother us anymore. This only causes further alienation.

- 28 -

DR. THOM PARK: THE KEYS TO SENIOR LEADERSHIP

Dr. Thom Park is a sport psychologist and leadership expert. Park is a former football coach and professor at Florida State University. He is the President of "Nehemiah's Wall at The Adirondack Center," an outdoor adventure school and team-building center for at-risk children and adults with mental retardation in St. Johnsville, N.Y.

Why is it so important for seniors to be the leaders of the team?

First, the role of seniors transcends simply the contributions they make as athletes. Sometimes, they don't understand that. As a coach, you may have to explain how they are centers of influence and key role models and that they need to act accordingly. Make them aware of that.

Second, the way you get responsibility out of people is to give them responsibility. If they can continue to progress in terms of readiness, being more able and more willing to act as role models and leaders on the team, then you give them more responsibility. What many of the great coaches have done increasingly in the last decade is to create management counsels on their team.

Describe a typical management counsel.

Their seniors meet with the head coach. The head coach talks about issues on the team and opens up lines of communication. It is not the dictatorship that it used to be a few decades ago. There is more democracy now then there ever was. What a management counsel does is give the players ownership of their team.

The coach can say, "this team is not going to be as good as I want it to be, but it is going to be as good as you want it to be."

So players have to take ownership in the process. If you give them responsibility of acting out those roles, you as the coach, are not the boss anymore. You have delegated some of that authority to them. The responsible person will elicit a positive response. The key here is to talk about the importance of leadership. By making them aware, you prepare them to delegate more tasks and responsibility.

What are some actions a coach can take if the seniors fail to live up to their responsibilities?

Mostly, you will simply tell them what to do. You treat them more like a child. As they exhibit the ability and willingness or an aptitude for behaving in a way that you sketched out for them, you can gradually add little bits of responsibility.

The ultimate threat is benching or termination. If you put somebody down on the second team, you are demoting him and essentially firing him for the week. You have ultimate authority. You have to look at how punishments tie in with motivation. That's your job. Great coaches are the people that are the psychologists who can figure out how to get into people's heads.

By saying just the right things and getting players to do certain things that they otherwise would not do is the mark of a great leader. The essence of coaching is getting inside people's heads and getting them to optimize when it counts, on game day. So you have many tools at your disposal to accomplish this.

One tool is the ultimate sanction of saying that, "You are not playing" or "You are kicked off the team." Now that will get a player's attention. But I would argue that you take more incremental steps before you drop the Trump card.

How about bypassing a poor senior class, and giving more responsibility to underclassmen, even making them team captains?

That is an interesting approach. You could easily find people that are juniors that have far more leadership abilities than the seniors that are not cutting it. I would argue that is not such a bad idea. If people have leadership ability, they should lead, regardless of age. I don't care whether they are seniors, juniors or whatever. If tradition has it that captains have to be seniors, that's fine. But if there is a void there, use common sense and put a leader in that capacity. Depart from tradition, and do the intelligent thing. How you handle this is unique to every team and every culture of every sport, keeping in mind what the traditions are and what the coaching management style is.

- 29 -

DR. JACK STARK, DR. HARVEY DULBERG, DR. KATE HAYES:
MAINTAINING FOCUS THROUGH ADVERSE LIFE CIRCUMSTANCES

Jack Stark (JS) is a former consultant for the University of Nebraska athletic program. Harvey Dulberg (HD) is a Boston based sports psychologist. Kate Hays (KH) is the president of the Performing Edge.

Tragic events pose a challenge for any sports team to stay focused while dealing with hardship. A team may not have a life-changing event like Hurricane Katrina, but they may have to deal with a parent's divorce or the loss of a loved one. Is it a good idea to dedicate a game or season's performance to the memory of a loved one who has passed away? Does that usually help or hinder an athlete's performance?

JS: Sometimes, I see this as media hype. I don't think it makes much of a difference one way or another. For example, the media blew up the fact that Roger Clemens pitched so soon after his mother passed away. It depends on the individual athlete. Dedicating a game to a loved one's memory can inspire one athlete, while another will have a difficult time concentrating.

HD: In the recent case of the New Orleans Saints first game of the year, the team may have felt like they were representing a region. They could provide a positive encouragement for those people from that area to feel good about. It seemed like the team came together and had a sense of purpose with their upset of the Carolina Panthers.

Athletes are part of a community where they compete. A guy like Joe Horn of the Saints was down at the Superdome handing out food. He dedicated himself to those people. For some athletes, tragic situations can provide an impetus to go out and be successful and perform at a higher level. The individual athlete can take out of the situation what they may- how they interpret the tragedy and how they grow from the experience is very individual. The best athletes have the ability to put away the distraction and then use it as a motivational tool.

What are some of the things that you would recommend athletes do during the grieving process that will help their on-field performance?

JS: I would recommend implementing a FOCUS technique. F stands for forget. O stands for organize. C stands for concentrate. U stands for unwind. S stands for swing or shot. This is a process athletes can use to give them structure and discipline. It helps athletes block out distractions. In a high pressure situation with the game on the line, the athlete needs to have the mind-set that, "Hey, I'm out here performing just like in practice- relaxed and focused." If they can follow this process every time they are about to take an at bat, shoot a free throw, kick a field goal or take a penalty shot, they get locked into a pattern where they won't be easily distracted. It's a practical routine that helps athletes regain focus during a game.

What role does a sport psychologist play to help the athlete refocus after a tragic event?

HD: At the professional or college level, if the athlete is anything less than 100% focused and 100% in the moment, he or she is not going to do well. If they are 2 miles an hour off on their fast ball or that pass goes inches over the receiver's head, those little mistakes can be the difference between winning and losing. The athlete has to have a place where they can talk about personal things that bother them with someone they trust and know that it stays in the sports psychologist's office. Then, that athlete can go out and do his or her thing.

Is there any kind of an organized plan you want the athlete to follow, or is it an individualized thing?

HD: I want everything to be choreographed, the same way that football coaches now have the first 25 plays choreographed or the basketball coach will choreograph the first five minutes of a game. I want to know exactly what the athlete is doing, and I want to know exactly what the athlete is thinking.

At any given moment, I want the athlete to know where they are mentally and physically. If they are not mentally there, we have strategies to get them where they should be.

If they start to think, "Oh my goodness, my neighbor died in the flood" or "Oh my wife is about to give birth and I should be there, but I have a basketball game to play," they may lose focus. We put in strategies to get them refocused.

Can you give an example of one strategy you may have helped somebody with?

HD: First, we find out when are the times the athlete tends to get distracted, so when the athlete is performing and gets off track, they have a cue to refocus themselves. The cue can be spitting on the hands before an at-bat or a pitcher writing inside his glove, "focus." The tennis player can tape on the top of their racket, "crush and destroy." They need a verbal expression that will help them refocus on the task at hand. My goal is to have the athletes catch themselves as soon as they start to drift and then have them use a cue as a way to refocus.

Dr. Stark, when you counseled the NASCAR team whom was dealing with the deaths of their teammates in a plane crash, what coping mechanisms helped them deal with their grief?

JS: As a clinical psychologist, I had a background helping people cope with death and dying. There was a staff of 500 on the team that were affected. People all go through grieving stages. First is shock. You can't believe it is happening. After a few days, stage two occurs, which is characterized by anger and hurt. People often stay in this stage for quite a while. Stage 3 is acceptance and moving forward. Sometimes people will struggle with depression as they move back and forth between stage 2 and 3.

Is there anything you can say or do to that person who is depressed?

JS: First, diagnose to see how many symptoms that person has. Second, you let them know what is normal and not normal.

Sometimes, I tell people that they are supposed to be depressed for a while. You went through a tragedy, and it's ok to grieve. If it lasts for a long time, sometimes an anti-depressant is needed. However, helping people build up the proper support system is the most important thing.

What is the role of faith in helping athletes keep their focus?

JS: Faith is a belief in things we can't always understand, feel, or touch. We can't understand why bad things are happening to us, but faith gives us hope that there is a greater purpose than what we can see. Especially for those who have been committed to their faith for a long period of time, they have a foundation that sustains them through trials.

On a lesser scale, many teams will deal with the loss of a team leader to season-ending injury. Do you have any recommendations on how the rest of the team can respond in a mentally tough manner?

JS: I like to use something called "the 5 percent technique." If there are 20 guys on a team, I will ask each one of them, "How many of you guys can give just five percent greater effort in the next game?" Invariably, they will all raise their hands. Then, I say, "There's 100 percent right there. You just replaced a guy. That's how we are going to make up for the loss of the other player. This isn't just going to happen easily. You will have to work harder, be more disciplined, and focus more. Now I know that you think you are already giving everything you've got, but if you dig down, you can give a little more." If each player feels like they have a small stake in the replacement of the star player, it gives them a goal to shoot for.

In sport, what does giving 5 percent effort look like?

JS: In football, 80 plays on offense and defense. If the athlete could make an extra effort and better execution on just four plays, that's 5 percent. Can you block harder and run harder for four more plays? I know you are going all out already, but pick four plays to take it to another level. Know they have a specific goal they can tie their performance to. I dedicate 4 plays to the loss of my injured teammate. It's easy to take a handful of plays off which leads to a penalty or something else bad happening.

In your experience of counseling people one-on-one, are there some coping mechanisms that have proved beneficial over the years? How do you help them block out distractions?

HD: It's a process. We talk about the ability to compartmentalize. Once the game is about to begin, there is nothing an athlete can do about a sick relative or a tragedy like the recent hurricanes. By compartmentalize, I mean to put away the personal issues and focus on the game for 3 hours.

Working with high school and college athletes, I say to them, "you can't be doing your math homework at practice. Conversely, when you are in the classroom, you can't be running a pass pattern in your mind. You have to be totally involved with what you are doing at the present moment."

For the athlete that means giving 100 percent to the team and to what their responsibility is. For the professional and college teams who have a sport psychologist on staff, they can provide a sounding board for the athlete. If the athlete speaks to a sport psychologist in the afternoon before a night game, they can "download" the personal problems to the counselor who helps clear the athlete's head so he/she can be ready to compete.

How can athletes learn to contain their emotions during these difficult times?

KH: The key to containing emotions is to heighten concentration. Here are examples of exercises or routines your athletes can try:

1. Use internal verbal messages to return concentration to the present moment. A single word, such as "strength" or "power" or a phrase such as "loose knees" can help your athlete focus on what is occurring and direct attention to specific elements of performance.

2. For some, a tangible memento is a helpful tool for concentration. These can be imbued with all the superstition and magic to which performers are prone to use. For example, after the death of their teammate Hank Gathers, Loyola Marymount basketball players wore a band with his name and number on their uniforms.

These mementos can be used to channel or focus concentration. Using the above example, it could have been suggested they touch the number to "put Hank's energy" into the next foul shot. That emotion-filled team went way beyond expectation in the NCAA tournament that year.

While these methods to increase momentary concentration are important, it is equally necessary to legitimize an atmosphere, which allows people to do the grieving work. Uncomfortable with our own or others sadness, we may try to comfort people with a dismissive attitude, saying something like, "Don't think about it. It's over." Much more useful would be a message that says, "Don't think about it now. We have a game to play. I'll support you in finding a time and a way to deal with it later." Public occasions such as memorials are one way of handling grief at a specific time and place.

Depending on the loss, there are private means to this end as well. Setting aside a specific time is important. The athletes should feel free to experience and sort through their emotions, whether with group discussions or alone in thought. Whether it is a physical or emotional loss, there are predictable feelings that a person will experience. Along with feelings of sadness, grief often includes disbelief, anger, and guilt before a person can experience a sense of resolution. Grief work occurs over a long period of time.

While each person needs to express loss with a combination of containment and grief, athletes handle their emotions individually. If you have also experienced this loss as a coach, it is equally important that you use this combination of methods to handle your own loss. This will serve your athletes in two ways- by dealing with your experience you will be available to help them more, and you will provide them with a model for coping with a loss.

- 30 -

Dr. Colleen Hacker: Producing Peak Performance Audio/Visual that Enhances Athlete Self-Motivation

Dr. Hacker is the sport psychology consultant for the U.S. Women's National Soccer team and co-author of the book "Catch Them Being Good".

What are the first steps a coach should take before attempting to produce a motivational type video?

The first questions you have to ask are, "Who is my audience? What is my purpose?"

Second, if you are devising peak performance audio/video/CDs/DVDs- you need to use the technology your athletes are most comfortable with. You need to become proficient in those technologies. That will represent a learning curve for most people. The structure of doing it can be a challenge. You won't get it perfect on the first try or maybe not the tenth try. But it will get better with each attempt.

Can you give an example of a specific motivational tape that you would produce?

Let's say you have come off a devastating loss. Now you have to play an opponent you haven't beaten recently. Let's say you're playing an opponent who beat you the last time out.

Maybe you are taking over a program that's been in the middle of the pack or down toward the bottom, and you want to build it to a league championship.

The purpose is to develop a motivational tool, but motivation for what? That becomes a second question. You want motivation to develop confidence in your team's abilities. Sometimes athletes are afraid of failing or afraid to look bad. They may even be afraid to succeed because even more will be expected of them.

Let's say you want to build confidence that an athlete can handle adversity; confidence that he or she will have the requisite skills to be successful, confidence that he or she can really handle the thrill and excitement that would come with this victory, confidence with our particular system, players, or style of play.

Once you're answered these questions, every answer leads to another question. What captures those feelings? What would make that message have more impact?

I have done motivational tapes that include little clips from movies or movie highlights; maybe it's something from "Remember the Titans" or "Searching for Bobby Fisher." Some people may think, "A chess movie?" but you'd be amazed at some of the scenes. Maybe it's something from "Thelma and Louise" or "Rocky." You want to infuse movie scenes that will capture your particular ethic or mood, and really drive home this message.

Another direction to go is where you tightly edit quality clips of your team making a basket, scoring the goal, stuffing the opponents defensively, or incurring floor burns because they're hustling after every ball or diving for a ball before it goes out over the touch line.

The movie clips by themselves can be unbelievably powerful and engaging. Another method is to combine the movie clips with tightly edited tapes of your own team, and your own players exhibiting this style, this skill, or this quality. Shorter is better than longer.

You want to capture people so that it's engaging, it's motivating, and it strikes at the heart, rather than the head. The messages should be subtle and powerful. There's a real art to it. That's why some move directors are better than others. The science is the technology. The art is how you apply the technology. The best coaches are skilled both at the art and the science of creating these tapes.

Do you think the coach needs to hire out a company to do this or have somebody on their own staff do it?

Somebody on his or her own staff can do it, but it takes time. On the national soccer team when I bring outside assistants to help me produce these tapes, it might take a year of practicing and working until we're all on the same page. It doesn't just happen overnight.

You have to know what you want. I think it's good to be mentored, but the staff can and should do a better job than hiring out a video production company, but only if they are willing to learn and do their homework.

In other words, the first ten tapes you make are probably not going to be good even though you're working you're butt off and you think you're doing a good job. There's a learning curve involved.

When I look at what I've done in the last year with nearly 10 years of experience, and compare them to some of the first tapes I made back in 1996, it's like a different person produced them.

Don't let the fact that your first ones aren't so good stop you. It's like anything else. You need to know what you're doing; you need to get professional advice, and coaching from someone who has done them before.

Nobody should know your athletes better than you. I think you're going to capture something that no one else can capture. This can be a very time intensive process. In 1996, the first tapes I made for the team and for individuals took me four hours to make a seven-minute tape. Multiply that by 20 players, and you understand the time involved.

Can you discuss the difference between imagery tapes and motivational tapes?

With imagery CD's/DVD's/tapes I've made for individual athletes, I want to create a mental skills training tool, not motivation. I want to help them improve their game. This isn't for motivation; this is for actual skill improvement.

When I'm going to make an imagery tape, what do I want to capture? What are all the different uses? I can do an imagery tape to help an athlete perfect skills or techniques that he or she has been working on. You can create an imagery tape to help athletes learn tactics, plays, or strategies.

For example, here we are changing the point of attack. Here we are in our match-up zone defense. Here's a player being able to execute a serve to perfection in a volleyball or tennis match.

There are many specific aspects of a player's game to work on-inbounds plays, rebounds, shooting, blocking out, one on one, zone, whatever it might be. The purpose is to instill confidence in a player's unique personality, imprinting this particular part of their game.

I do imagery tapes for athletes coming back from injuries, so they understand what strengths they have, and their triumphs and their accomplishments. You can create imagery tapes for a lot of different outcomes.

These should be extremely individual, personal, tailor-made and unique. It's generally helpful to include athlete-selected music as the backdrop, but I also use raw footage as well. When you have 90,000 people cheering- that's a pretty powerful audio message as well.

What about team versus individual tapes?

Generally, the most positive benefits come from individually created tapes. I also create team-oriented tapes as well. In my experience, I would want every individual to have their own before I'd want to do one for the whole team.

You can create a team tape following the same principles. Here's us being successful against big-time opponents. Here's us using the strategy successfully that we're going to need to use in Saturdays' game. Here's us triumphing against this opponent that we've never beaten before because that's what we're going to do in this upcoming game.

99% of human beings can find people who are better at what they do than themselves to model.

For example, a soccer player would be able to get images of the men and women's national team players executing a play to perfection.

The problem is when you're working with an athlete that's already the best at what they do. There are fewer "mastery models" available.

What are some of those different ways you have to adjust your strategy when working with the best of the best?

In individual tapes, I will show them performing their signature moves, their signature strengths and skills. I want to show them at their best. I will pick from a very small number of players in the world who on a particular skill, technique, or event, these top elite athletes would find worthy of respect.

If you're the best in the world at what you do, then you only want to hear from other people who are the best in the world at what they do. It's not unusual for me to show the elite soccer players that I work with a major league baseball player who is an all star or an NBA champion athlete. They can relate to that. There are not many people that have faced what our athletes have faced at this level.

If you're a high school coach in the state play-offs, then showing your team a college tape of the NCAA division one finals would be a step up. If you are a division one NCAA division championship team coach, then showing your team the national team would be a step up. If you're the third best team in the world, then show clips of someone that's the best at their particular sport.

- 31 -

DR. TONI ZIMMERMAN: CONSIDERATIONS FOR MEN COACHING WOMEN ATHLETES

Toni Zimmerman is a marriage and family studies professor at Colorado State University. She formerly was a sport psychology consultant to athletic teams using family therapy techniques to build team unity.

Address the motivational differences between men and women athletes and what a coach should be aware of.

Women don't tend to respond as well in a rigid hierarchy as they do in a flat hierarchy. So obviously the coach is at the top of the hierarchy. Management guru Pat Himes talks about how boys from the time they are very young, are socialized to always have somebody in charge. A team player, a coach- even their play is very much coordinated with somebody who is in charge. Whereas girls traditional kind of play that we grew up with corresponds more to a circle. There is not somebody in charge. In fact it is just the opposite. So they don't tend to respond real well to real rigid hierarchy.

Having an attitude of "I am in charge and you are not" will cause women to not respond well. They respond a lot better with an approach that says, "These are the ideas that I have, what are your ideas? This is what I'm thinking about doing, what do you think about that?"

Women in general will respect the hierarchy and let the coach be in charge, but far more if they feel like they have a say, that they are important, and that they are on the team. Women need positive reinforcement and choices- they need to feel like they are a part of what is going on.

They don't respond well to an approach of, "just shut up and listen to what I am saying, don't ask questions." They just have not been socialized that way. Women respond better to dialogue, communication, getting some choices, and having some say. So any way in which you can flatten the hierarchy while still being the bottom line, is very helpful.

How can male coaches build rapport with female athletes?

They should be up front about gender differences, sex roles, and sexism. There are two kinds of differences that exist in our world between males and females. One is simply gender differences. That is to say, "Men are more like this and women are more like that." For instance women may tend to be more nurturing. Males tend to be more instrumental and narrowly focused.

But the male coach should talk honestly with females about the sexism that exists within society. It has certainly changed over the years, but there is still a long way to go. Women still hold less power positions or important positions in our society.

If a male coach can just demonstrate that he understands that situation, he will improve his relationship with team members.

Let's say the team gets into a situation where they have less fans of the game than their male counterparts. Many times women athletes will internalize that in a negative way. They will think they are not good enough rather than realizing that society heavily promotes male sports. It is going to take a long time for people to be as interested in the average female team as they are in the average male team.

It is very frustrating for female athletes to get up in the morning and read all about male teams who may be winning far less games, but get twice the media coverage.

If females can feel like a male coach understands their situation, then when you deal with issues like lack of media coverage or low attendance, you can really talk about that through the lens of sexism in society versus a team internalizing that into how good, popular, or entertaining they are.

- 32 -

DR. ALAN GOLDBERG: A GROUNDBREAKING APPROACH TO SLUMPBUSTING

Dr. Goldberg is a sport psychologist who helps athletes get out of slumps. He is the author of "Sports Slump Busting" and "This is Your Brain on Sports: Beating Blocks, Slumps, and Performance Anxiety for Good".

What is the most common problems athletes are having?

They have specific performance problems such as choking, not playing up to their potential, experiencing fears and blocks, and those who can't seem to break through to the next level for whatever reason. These athletes have ruled out physical causes or technique issues for their performance problems. It's clearly a problem between their ears.

What's the latest you are doing with athletes in regards to slumps?

I'm working with Dr. David Grand, a Long Island psychologist who is doing break-through work in the area of performance psychology. He's completely changed the way I work with athletes. I now believe that every performance problem has a trauma base. It doesn't have to be a significant, capital "T" trauma. But if you look carefully at the athlete's history you will find one or more past injuries or emotional traumas- related or unrelated to their sport- that form the foundation of performance problems later.

Here is one example- A Division 1 softball pitcher is having control problems. She is flinching on the mound. She didn't even realize that she was doing it. Her problem is that she is afraid of getting hit. As a senior in high school, she got hit in the head with a ball that was hit right back at her. It subsequently freaked her out. She has carried around that trauma for well over a year now.

Another example- A college goalkeeper I worked with was tentative in the net. Certain game conditions would make him more nervous- rainy days for instance. He could handle the ball kicked way to his left or right, or way above his head. When a direct shot was hit right at him, he would bobble the ball. In his history, I learned that he had some injuries including a broken hand and times he was kicked in the head. But the worst memory of all happened to him in high school. From the sidelines, he watched the All State, senior keeper get kicked hard in the head and sent to the hospital. That memory had stuck with him.

For the pitcher I just mentioned, her experience was very close to consciousness. The goalkeeper wasn't even close to thinking about his past events. He wasn't worried about getting hurt, but nevertheless he was still very nervous and tentative.

What happens with these athletes is that the trauma experience doesn't get "digested" like other normal experiences will. It gets frozen in the athlete's mind and body. The body develops a memory of the past traumas. Whether the athlete is conscious of them or not is totally irrelevant. These scary experiences can then get stacked, one on top of another. When the athlete is in a similar situation or simply under pressure, components of that original trauma (images, emotions, physical sensations or negative thoughts) get activated and interfere with present performance.

Examples of the trauma showing itself include images of the past experiences flashing in the athlete's mind, nervousness, tension, jitteriness, shakiness, and negative thoughts. The root causes of a performance slump are these small traumas that have built up over the years and reached a critical mass. Every time an athlete experiences a trauma- it could be something small like taking a hard hit on the boards in hockey or colliding with a catcher in baseball- it gets filed away in the athlete's mind and body.

Then the athlete sprains an ankle; next they get embarrassed by a coach in front of teammates. Finally, they get hit with a pitch. At some point, which is different for every athlete, that one more recent trauma or event becomes the straw that breaks the camel's back.

All of the sudden, a performance problem pops up. To the people looking in from the outside- teammates, coaches, parents- it might not make any sense at all. Nothing really bad seemed to happen to John or Jane. However, the performance problem that has emerged is the sum of all of these past traumas.

Seeing performance problems from this perspective has changed the way I work with athletes. Most sport psychologists, myself included, will work on the specific aspects of a performance problem. If an athlete has a performance block or fear, I look at what their self-talk is (what they say to themselves), and what are they focusing on before or during the performance. These factors can cause stress, which causes muscles to tighten up, and breathing to get erratic. Then you can't perform well, which leads to a slump. However, looking at an athlete's conscious mental strategies is really only scratching the surface of the problem. It's not directly addressing the problem's roots- the underlying traumas.

So what would you say to an athlete to help them get over the problem?

First, it's not about what I would say to an athlete. Coaches and teammates often tell a kid, "hey, you don't have anything to worry about, you'll be fine. Your injury was a freak experience. It won't happen again."

The athlete can't really use this conscious reassurance. Telling them that they have nothing to worry about or that they can do this, does not get through to the underlying fear.

This is because the athlete who is dealing with a past trauma is dealing with a body memory that is mostly out of their control. Before I started working with Dr. Grand and his version of EMDR, I could help some athletes with their problems, but not others. I never knew why I couldn't make a dent in certain athlete's problems. Now I know. The reason was that the roots of their performance problem went far deeper than their surface mental toughness strategies.

Briefly explain the EMDR (eye movement desensitization and repro-

cessing) method you and Dr. Grand use with athletes.

First off, the work that we do goes far beyond traditional EMDR. EMDR was developed in the late 1980's to help people who suffer from PTSD (Post Traumatic Stress Disorder). It utilizes bi-lateral stimulation of the brain to help the individual separate their traumatic emotions and physical reactions from the memory of the experience. Bilateral stimulation of the brain means having an athlete alternate left to right eye movements (sitting still and looking straight ahead, the athlete would move their eyes two feet to the left and then two feet to the right. The eye movement back and forth is called bi-lateral stimulation.) I also have athletes listen to a special CD designed by Dr. Grand that goes in their left ear, then their right ear- back and forth. It has wave sounds and acoustic guitars. (See page 7).

How exactly does this help an athlete with a performance slump?

Combing bi-lateral stimulation of the brain with components of the original trauma (images, emotions, physical reactions, and negative thinking), the athlete can process through the past traumatic experience. It is very similar to work done with soldiers who experience post-traumatic stress disorders after war. This isn't talk therapy. We're not just rehashing the feared experience over and over again.

Here's what happens- the more an athlete processes a past experience in this way, the less connected the emotion and physical reactions are to the memory.

For example, let's say a kid has a fear reaction about getting kicked in the head and they cringe when placed in certain pressure situations. The fear reaction will get less and less over time along with the jittery body responses. Ultimately, the athlete will go back to the bad memory and they will say, "hey that's all in the past." They lose the residual reaction of fear and the body reaction (muscle tension).

Athletes who have had serious injury must deal with two things: 1) The emotion of the injury, which reveals itself in "butterflies" in the stomach and 2) Physical sensations around the area that had been injured.

The goal of EMDR is to disconnect and get that bad body memory out of the mind and also disconnect the negative emotions associated with the past trauma. What's left is simply a normal past memory for the athlete.

What is your advice to coaches and parents who have an athlete who is experiencing a slump?

They need to be patient and reassuring. The last thing they need to do is focus on outcomes and increasing the pressure. The worst thing to do with kids who are struggling is to get angry with them or accuse them of willfully not trying hard enough.

No serious athletes want to struggle with or have performance problems. Do they want their coaches and parents to be frustrated with them? Of course not.

In many instances, coaches start feeling frustrated because they can't help the kid. After they have tried everything and they can't crack the kid- they turn up the pressure and threaten. But that is the worst thing to do. You want to be supportive. You want to understand the problem. It's not like the kid wants to be nervous or wants to choke.

- 33 -

DR. KEN RAVIZZA: MASTERING PERFORMANCE CYCLES TO MAINTAIN ABSOLUTE CONCENTRATION

Ravizza is a pioneer in the field of sport psychology. Author of "Heads Up Baseball", he has worked with Olympic, NFL, Major League baseball teams, and collegiate national champions in baseball, softball and gymnastics.

How important is it for athletes to take responsibility for their own performance? Let's look at an example of a tennis player who just double faulted. He's ticked off, but now he has to move over to the other side of the court. How should this athlete handle him or herself mentally?

Responsibility is the concept that engulfs the whole performance cycle concept. If you're not going to take responsibility for your performance, you can forget everything else we're going to discuss here. Basically you are saying, "My performance is out of my control and is being handled by the cosmic forces."

Once the athlete is willing to take responsibility, then he or she has got to do some things: 1. Recognize where I am. I just double faulted, I'm pissed off. It could also be that double faulting was okay, because those were two very good serves. I've got to stick with it; it's going to be okay.

The person has to decide where are they are mentally. I like to use a signal light analogy. Green light is go, yellow is watch out, red is be ready to stop and regroup.

What are some questions athletes should ask themselves to find out where they are mentally?

What do you experience when the garbage is hitting the fan for you? When do I start to spin out of control? What happens in your body in terms of heart rate, blood pressure, and muscle tension? What happens in terms of your thoughts? Do you lose focus? Do you start doubting yourself? What happens to your behavior? Do you slow down or speed up? These are all great questions to help the athlete quickly recognize where they are.

Okay, let's get back to the tennis player. Talk about the release phase.

They have 30 seconds from when the point is scored until they have to serve again. They have a 30 second window to work things out.

Here is the mindset. I just double faulted. I've already got negative self-talk going. I know I have to do something to release it and let it go. How do I let go of it and release it? The release may be picking up the ball, turning around to walk back to where I'm going to serve and saying a favorite phrase.

I may grip the racquet and squeeze to release and blow off some steam. Now I have to step over to that point where I'm done with that last serve. The athlete may squeeze the racquet, walk back to the cage area and have a spot to look at. Looking at that spot reminds me to stand tall, get ready and focused. Now I step to the line, I'm good and ready.

What happens to the athlete during the refocus and ready phase?

What do I need to do right now? What's my plan? Once I have my plan, I need to commit to it. If I'm going to do this type of serve, commit to doing it. Don't just sort of see what happens. A key part of having a good plan and refocusing is the commitment that goes to the plan.

Once I have my plan and I know what I'm doing, I want to make sure I'm ready. How do I know I'm ready? I can breathe. Inhale. Exhale. It's a trusting breath.

There may be a breath earlier when I just double faulted when I exhale, blow it out and let it go. Then I turn around, I regroup and refocus. Now, I'm committed to what I'm going to do. Inhale. Exhale. Then execute.

How about taking us through the same cycle we just did with a quarterback in football who just finished a play?

The play is over. The whistle blows, he recognizes that "I blew it" if the play was unsuccessful. He's got a yellow or a red light. If he did great, he just gets up and goes. Either way, he is going to have to come to the point where he can recognize where he is mentally.

Let's say he blew it. He needs to do something to release and let go of the preceding play- maybe picking up some dirt, throwing it down. It may be un-strapping his chin strap.

Then what he needs to do is regroup and refocus. As he gets closer to the huddle, he needs to get himself together in terms of the way he's carrying and handling himself. When he's in the huddle, he needs to look to the sideline to get the play. He's going through his thought process.

The problem with quarterbacks is that they carry the last play with them, and they don't think clearly. He's got to let go of that last play before the next play- even if it was a good play.

It's much easier with a good play because you go right to refocus. You don't have to release anything or regroup. You're okay. Lights are green, go to refocus, next play.

But if lights are yellow or red, then they've got to release some mental baggage. I like to use cues like un-strapping the chinstrap. I like triggers.

Now, he steps into the huddle and says to his teammates, "Ready."

"Ready" basically means everyone looks at him. Everyone's right there mentally. The first thing that you need to do as a quarterback is to make sure you have everyone's attention. The inexperienced quarterback will come in the huddle and start spitting out the play and half the players aren't even looking at him and half the players aren't listening. He first needs to get the players' attention.

Ready, eye contact, we're going to do this play. Now the information is given. Then he breaks the huddle. Inhale. Exhale. As he walks up to the line of scrimmage, he needs to be reading the defense. So he's picking up some cues. His energy has to be outwardly focused. If he's into "I gotta do this or that" or he's cussing about the last play, he's not going to read the defense as well.

Now, he comes up to the line of scrimmage. I encourage quarterbacks to inhale and exhale as they come out of the huddle. Take a good breath right there. Some of them may take another breath as they put their hands under the center. The play is executed. Move on to the next play. If I screwed up, I've got to release some stuff before I get back to the huddle. So the play begins in the huddle, it doesn't begin at the line of scrimmage. That is an important concept to emphasize.

When I worked with Nebraska football for three years under former coach Tom Osborne, he said that I could help him out on two related issues.

First, when our players make a mistake, they hold on to it. Second, we've got to get better focus in the huddle. We went through this with the staff and the first day of fall ball after the guys had stretched. Tom brought them down to the end zone, and I sat out there and we basically went through forming the huddle. We went through what happens right after the whistle just blew the last play dead. Your job is to be present when you get back to the huddle. If you have to release stuff, do it, but when you get in that huddle we need you there- mentally ready.

You often hear about players being fine in non-pressure situations, but tightening up and "choking" when stakes get higher. How can athletes prevent this from happening?

The issue becomes, "where does the breakdown in performance occur?" Is the person failing to recognize it? Do they recognize and then not release? Do they regroup? How is their body language? Are they refocused? Are they thinking clearly, and committed to what they are going to do? Are they trusting themselves and just doing it?

The key is to find where the mental breakdown occurs. This is where the coach has to find out what's going on. That's the coach's role or the sports psychologist's role.

Can the player go through the 4 R's? Can they keep them in the right sequence? The routine functions to give athletes something to do consciously. If we're going through the light signals, all the negative stuff has a much lesser chance of entering the mind and interfering with performance.

I want the routine to be conscious. I do not want the routine to be automatic. Once a routine is automatic, it's a habit pattern. The routine is something athletes go through to get themselves where they need to be mentally.

If the lights are green, I'm just going, it's pretty much just automatic. So if the signal is green, go forward, it's no big deal. If it's yellow, I've got to do other things.

A lot of athletes say that to me, well I do this or that and it's automatic. Well if it's automatic, then by definition you can do it without thinking about it. This means then you can do it without beating yourself up.

Performance routines or cycles can't come from a coach by telling the athlete what he or she needs to do. It needs to be their thing.

Let's look at the open sports (those with constant movement and limited breaks in the action). In field or ice hockey, basketball, soccer or lacrosse, you have players running up and down a court or field. They are not going to have time to go through a full performance cycle, but the same procedure still takes place, just at a much quicker pace. What is your advice for these athletes?

Soccer players have told me I'm used to working with baseball players, but "our world is a very quick world." What they are really saying is this, "I can do it (the performance cycle), but it's going to be a much faster process."

Let's take a look at ice hockey, which has shifts. Players come out, then they recognize where they are. They may be ticked off a little because of what just happened on the ice.

This is the point where they can release it, pound the stick or whatever. Then, regroup by the way you start sitting. Get your shoulders up, sternum up, you start getting into the flow of the game. Now you are ready for the next shift.

Also, take the classic example in basketball. How many times do you see someone come down on a fast break, blow the lay-up, then reach in and foul the guy? It's so common because the guy's out of control and he's pissed off. If the player is mentally tough, what should happen after he or she blows the lay up is that he/she has to hustle back on defense.

As the player runs back, this is the time to bad mouth yourself, say a negative comment, make a fist, and then release it. Once you turn around, you're now on defense. There's that old concept of turning around, both physically and in your mind.

As the athlete sprints back, the ball's down court in the far corner. I back off my man, I'm communicating with my guys, the ball starts moving around as it gets closer to my area, I get pulled towards the ball. So the ball is dictating where I'm at mentally.

In water polo, we used to talk to the guys about what to do after they missed a shot. Since they have to go under water, take this opportunity to just kick hard, and release that poor shot. When they pop their head back up out of the water, they should be ready for the next play.

In all of the ball sports, the thing the athletes focus on is the ball. The ball is their direction. It's them and the ball. It's the athlete and the space, in relation to the ball, that becomes critical. The mental transition in soccer takes place on the offense-defense switch. As a soccer player hustles back on defense, he or she needs to figure out what they need to do in relation to the ball. That is their concentration cue to focus on.

In baseball or softball, the ball is a last minute deal. It's the batters box that's critical. The batter's box is what you get into. That's where I get my focus. That's the last thing before you're going to make a hit. When I'm out of the box, I don't need to be focused. I go in and out. There's more time for that process of the 4 R's to take place.

Talk a little bit about getting uncomfortable with being comfortable. Is that the same thing as letting go of mistakes?

What does being comfortable do for us as athletes? Comfortableness feeds our confidence. When we have confidence, we trust our ability. Confidence gives us trust. What happens when our confidence isn't there?

Confidence isn't all or none. It runs on a continuum. There are some days we've got it all, some days we have very little, and some days when it's in between.

I think too many athletes get so caught up into wanting to be "in the zone" and wanting to feel "perfect" every play, that they miss out and miss the bigger point. Let's face facts. An athlete is in the zone maybe 10 or 15 percent of the time, if they are lucky.

The issue is what are they going to do with the other 85 to 90 percent of the time?

I say this to athletes, "So what if you're not feeling good? You have to learn how to deal with it. Stop dwelling on not feeling right and think of what you have to do to get better. Focus on what you need to do right now."

One of the reasons coaches are so into fundamentals is that they are like the life jacket when the garbage hits the fan. Fundamentals are what you go to get yourself back together after a mistake.

The concept of getting comfortable with being uncomfortable is all about getting into the present moment. I've got to focus on the process, and I've got to be as positive as I can be with it.

Example: In the past when I've worked with a team, I would say to them, "Starting now for the next 30 seconds, I want you to listen intently. I want you to be totally focused. OK, right now, you're listening to me differently than you were just a few moments before. You're now doing something differently than you were eight seconds ago. This is what turning things around is about. The way you turn it around is for a few seconds you just lock into what you are doing wrong and then figure out what you need to do to get back on track. Peak performance is all about refocusing, more than focusing. It's all about coming back to what you need to do- right here, right now."

WINNING THE ATHLETIC MENTAL GAME

Book Order Form

☐   Yes, I want additional copies of "Winning the Athletic Mental Game"

• 1 copy: $45.   • 2-4 copies: $35 each.   • 5-9 copies: $30 each.
• 10 - 19: $25 each.   • 20 or more $22 each.

Shipping and handling is free for any size order.

# of copies_____ Order total_____

☐ Check enclosed. (Please make payable to: Championship Performance)

Charge my credit card: ☐ Visa   ☐ Master Card   ☐ American Express
                                ☐ Discover Card

Acct number:_____ Expiration date:_____

☐ Bill my organization. (Paperwork and PO # must accompany order.)

Ship to:

Name:_____

Organization:_____

Address: _____

City:_____ State_____ Zip_____

Return to:
Championship Performance
10612 - D Providence Road Suite 262
Charlotte, NC 28277

Or order by phone:
Toll free 1-877-465-3421 or (704) 321-9198
FAX: (704) 321-0203
Web: www.championshipperform.com

Made in the USA
Charleston, SC
23 July 2013